orexi!

orexi!

FEASTING AT THE MODERN GREEK TABLE

THEO A. MICHAELS

PHOTOGRAPHY BY MOWIE KAY

RYLAND PETERS & SMALL

LONDON • NEW YORK

Dedication
For my yiayias and papous

Senior Designer Sonya Nathoo
Editors Julia Charles and
Kate Reeves-Brown
Production David Hearn
Art Director Leslie Harrington
Editorial Director Julia Charles
Publisher Cindy Richards

Food Stylist Kathy Kordalis
Prop Stylist Tony Hutchinson
Indexer Hilary Bird

First published in 2019
by Ryland Peters & Small
20–21 Jockey's Fields
London WC1R 4BW
and
Ryland Peters & Small
341 E 116th St
New York NY 10029
www.rylandpeters.com

Text © Theo A. Michaels 2019.

Design and commissioned photographs
© Ryland Peters & Small 2019. See
page 176 for full picture credits.

ISBN: 978-1-78879-079-6

10 9 8 7 6 5 4 3 2 1

Printed and bound in China.

CIP data from the Library of Congress
has been applied for.
A CIP record for this book is available
from the British Library.

Important Notes for Cooks

* Extra-virgin olive oil is the highest
quality oil. It is unrefined, contains
antioxidants and anti-inflammatories and
has a low smoke point and heightened
flavour. It is best used for dressings and
drizzles. Refined olive oil is milder in
flavour and contains less health benefits
but its higher smoke point makes it good
for cooking. I use Aloades olive oil from
a family owned business in Cyprus.

* Both British (metric) and American
(imperial plus US cups) are included in
these recipes; however, it is important
to work with one set of
measurements and not alternate
between the two.

CONTENTS

EAT LIKE A GREEK 6

YOGURT & PITA 8
Yiaourti kai pita

MEZE 10
Meze

SEA 44
Thalassa

LAND 70
Gi

SUN 98
Ilios

FIRE 128
Fotia

SUNDOWNERS 154
Thysi iliou

INDEX 174

ACKNOWLEDGEMENTS
& PICTURE CREDITS 176

EAT LIKE A GREEK

In the following pages you'll discover Greek and Cypriot-inspired recipes. Some are born out of childhood memories, others from professional kitchens, more than a few stem from an urgent need to whip up something fast to feed a rabble of hungry kids, and others from those precious lazy weekends when cooking for friends and family is as therapeutic as it is fun. This book contains, and I quote, 'the best Greek recipes ever written in the history of Greek cuisine' (thanks Mum). Many of the dishes may, of course, be familiar to lovers of Greek food, while others are my own new creations. Some recipes are inspired by simple village food rarely experienced outside the Greek community, others are creations that my own family cook; not found in a Greek taverna but frequently present on our kitchen table.

The Greek diet is regarded as one of the healthiest in the world, largely due to the high content of vegetables, fruit, grains, pulses, seafood, olive oil and also fermented dairy foods like live yogurt and feta cheese, but I think eating like a Greek is more than that – it is a life philosophy. It's about maintaining a balanced way of eating and living that is sustainable and not adhering to the concept of a prescribed 'diet'. Too much of anything isn't good but not enough of some foods is just as bad. I've never liked the idea of a diet full of rules. I find no love or sensuality in that and, quite frankly, it strips away all the pleasure of eating for me. My own food philosophy originates from village life. My mother grew up in Cyprus and her family grew most of their own produce as their main source of sustenance; leeks, pulses, chard, beetroot, potatoes, tomatoes, cucumbers, figs, dates and so on. They also kept a small number of livestock; pigeons, rabbits, even the odd turkey. They ate meat in moderation, maybe once a week, usually on a Sunday and even then it was mostly chicken. At the time, this way of living was simply born out of necessity; eating what you cultivated was frugality at its best and provided the means to feed a family. Things have changed a lot in Cyprus since then with the abundance of processed foods and use of agricultural chemicals, but ironically, a couple of generations later back in the UK and I'm trying to eat and feed my family with organic, local and sustainable produce as if it's a new idea.

And what actually is Greek food? What makes something Greek? Contrary to popular belief, just adding feta to something doesn't cut it (see page 102 for me just adding feta to make something Greek...). But is Greek food simply defined by its ingredients? For sure, there are a handful of foods that are exclusive plus there are specific dishes like *saganaki* and *kleftiko* but the headline flavours of lemon, thyme, oregano and olive oil that lace so many of our dishes and are indigenous to the land aren't exclusive to us (albeit they are the world's best, I'm just saying...). Other ingredients like pasta and rice may be associated more with Italy or China but have been used in Greek and Cypriot cuisine for centuries. Every nation that has ever been invaded has been left with an indelible mark on its culture and cuisine. Ingredients and seasonings from all around the globe are now available in every 'world food' aisle in your supermarket and previously unknown cooking methods have been popularized, meaning the food we all eat is constantly evolving. Right now, incredibly talented Greek and Cypriot chefs are pushing the boundaries of what we define as Greek cuisine today, but it most likely won't be how we define it 100 years from now. And nor should it be.

Personally, I believe the heritage of Greek food is not

wouldn't have the essence of a Cypriot dinner. Alone, we may eat frugally, but we entertain BIG. So hospitality and abundance for sure, but it's also the stories that cradle a plate of food, the childhood memory of eating something all together and the conversations around a table. Ultimately, I would define Greek food as honest, made from wonderful produce, rooted in village life, but made with a passion that Greeks can barely hide. The epitome of this, for me, is the Greek salad, probably one of the simplest to create, the difficulty lies in restraint. Its beauty lies in letting its ingredients shine. The ripest tomatoes, juicy cucumbers, sharp red onions, creamy feta, tangy olives, heady dried oregano, a drizzle of golden olive oil and a splash of sharp vinegar. Food of the Gods.

I wrote this book not intending to set out rigid instructions but to provide a template for you to work within, and that I hope will inspire you to add your own touches. I've shared my recipes and knowledge, but ultimately food should be enjoyed, and if that means adding a little more of this or a little less of that to suit your preferences, then please go ahead. It's the nuances and personality of each cook that is the magic ingredient. A heavy hand, a light hand, is precisely what gives each dish its own DNA, what makes one mother's *moussaka* different from another's. I tend to use drizzles and glugs, a pinch of this and a handful of that and I want you to feel comfortable doing the same, don't overthink it and have fun. I am hoping to come across copies of this book transformed into a cook's crime scene with blood-red beetroot stains and olive oil fingerprints – a cookbook should be well-used.

Oh, and if you're wondering... Orexi comes from the Greek *Kali Orexi*, meaning good appetite, a bit like saying the French *Bon Appetit!*, only louder. Theo x

simply about the ingredients, but is a combination of the people, their lands and history and the adaptability of a nation that are all bound by an unbroken thread woven through the tapestry of Greek and Cypriot culture. The legends and myths that Greeks do so well become entwined with the cuisine, lashing romance and history, sometimes nostalgia around each recipe. It's about the famed Greek hospitality that lingers in every dish, the habit of making enough for 10 when only 5 are coming to dinner. It's about abundance; we feed everyone – it's how we show our love, and how I show mine. (Though my wife has commented that diamonds work just as well...) Anyone who knows a Greek, knows hospitality; no one goes hungry. Having dinner at a Greek home with just enough for everyone,

YOGURT & PITA BREAD
yiaourti kai pita

Both yogurt and pita are synonymous with Greek and Cypriot cuisines and an everyday staple. Though styles may vary slightly from country to country, region to region and household to household, they are all in essence just simple recipes of humble origin that are still as popular today as they were thousands of years ago. I find a romance in making both, following processes that are as old as Greek civilization itself, and then finally devouring the fruits of my labour and tasting a little bit of history.

I am sharing the recipes I use at home here. You'll notice in the yogurt recipe I give very precise temperatures, which is something I fundamentally dislike doing... But I've made it a ton of times and rarely hit them exactly, so don't be put off as a little variation is okay. Also, as a rule, the longer you leave your yogurt fermenting, the sharper it will taste; personally, I think about 5 hours is good but it is up to you.

Pita for me is synonymous with family barbecues and it almost feels as vital to proceedings as the charcoal! A little insider knowledge: if you ever find yourself at a Greek barbecue, keep a look out for a conspicuous looking kitchen towel that's warm to the touch with yeast-scented steam seeping out... that is where you'll find the pita!

HOMEMADE YOGURT
ellinko yiaourti

Making your own yogurt is extremely easy and surprisingly satisfying. To kick-start the process, I use yogurt with 'live active cultures'. Besides being good for you, they also do the job of speeding up the fermentation process.

2 litres/quarts full-fat/whole milk
70 g/^{1}/$_3$ cup active live natural/plain yogurt

a thermometer
MAKES ABOUT 750 G/3^1/$_2$ CUPS

Warm the milk in a large saucepan to just under boiling point; do this slowly to avoid a grainy textured yogurt. Keep stirring to avoid it burning at the bottom of the pan. You want the thermometer to read about 93°C/200°F. Once you've hit that temperature, remove from the heat and let it cool to about 45°C/115°F.

Mix 250–500 ml/1–2 cups of the warm milk into the yogurt, and then tip the lot back into the pan with the rest of the milk and whisk. Cover with a lid and let it ferment for about 5 hours at 43°C/110°F. You can do this in the oven with the light on or in a warm spot in the kitchen.

After the 5 hours is up, transfer the pan to the fridge to cool and set. Once chilled, decant it into a sterilized jar and it will keep for a couple of weeks. If this regular yogurt doesn't float your boat and you want something more unctuous, then I suggest you go Greek! Which is just a simple case of straining... Line a colander with some muslin/cheesecloth, pour in the yogurt, tie the ends of the cloth and put the colander in a saucepan in the fridge. Leave for 1–2 hours until you have thick and creamy yogurt.

LEAVENED FLATBREAD
pita

Light, fluffy Cypriot-style pita is traditionally thinner and cooked until the steam inside puffs up and creates a stuffable pocket. To keep these supple, envelop them in a kitchen towel while they are still hot from the oven.

400 g/3 cups plain/all-purpose flour, plus extra
for dusting
a 7-g/¹/₄-oz. sachet dried active yeast
2 generous pinches of sugar
2 generous pinches of salt
2 tablespoons olive oil
250 ml/1 cup warm water

MAKES 8

Preheat the oven to 230°C (450°F) Gas 8 with a baking sheet inside.

Sift 340 g/2¹/₂ cups of the flour into a mixing bowl and add the yeast, sugar and salt. Mix briefly. Drizzle over the olive oil and pour in the warm water. Gently mix everything together into a 'shaggy mess' with a wooden spoon. Knead this 'mess' for about 5 minutes. If it's too sticky, add the remaining flour and keep kneading until fully incorporated. Once the dough has a springy texture, pop it in a lightly oiled bowl and cover with a kitchen towel. Leave for at least 45 minutes and up to 2 hours to rise; it should double in size and be extremely light and aerated. Knock the air out of it and divide into 8 balls. Flatten with the palm of your hand, cover with a damp cloth and let rest for 15 minutes. Roll each ball to 5 mm/¹/₄ inch thick, quickly place the pitas onto the hot baking sheet and back into the oven as quickly as possible to avoid losing heat. Once puffed up with steam, they are done.

UNLEAVENED FLATBREAD
pita horis zymi

Unleavened bread is made without any raising agents, such as yeast, so this recipe couldn't be easier or quicker. These Greek-style pitas are soft and pliable and great for wrapping around meats and salad.

215 g/1 cup Greek yogurt
260 g/2 cups plain/all-purpose flour, plus extra
for dusting
1 tablespoon olive oil
salt
butter, for cooking

MAKES 6

Add the yogurt, flour and olive oil to a bowl with a pinch of salt, and mix with a wooden spoon to combine everything.

Then knead with your hands until a soft dough ball appears. It will seem too dry at first, but persevere, and add a little more yogurt or flour if needed.

Cut the dough into six pieces. Roll out each piece to 5 mm/¹/₄ inch thick. I usually fry these in a frying pan/skillet on a medium heat in a little butter (but you can use dash of olive oil if you like) for a couple of minutes on each side.

Once cooked, wrap in a kitchen towel to keep warm or let them cool; either way they're great.

Tip: If you want more gyro-style flatbreads but don't have the time (or inclination) to make pitas from scratch, you can add a heaped teaspoon of baking powder to the flour in this recipe at the start; it won't officially be unleavened but is a good 'cheat' to know!

meze

MEZE
meze

We have all come together to eat, family and friends, a sacred occasion but not a rare one. This time the congregation is eating out at a local taverna, one of many in North London, amidst the Cypriot community living in the neighbourhood. The word taverna is derived from the latin *taberna* which can mean inn, shop, shed or even workshop and I rather like the romantic notion that the latter is exactly what it is. A cook's workshop, where they can fine-tune their offerings for their dining guests' pleasure. Nothing too pretentious, just good food cooked in a traditional way.

We enter the taverna and walk to the table, all of us urgently strategizing where to sit – you only have a few seconds so the pressure is immense. Yiayias and bapous have an automatic rank of seniority that only comes with age and instantly dictates their seats but the young (basically the army privates of any Greek family) who have not yet earned their stripes are not given a choice. The old with the old, the young with the young. If you procrastinate too long you may get a seat

in the wrong division, but that's okay – you'll jump to another one as soon as a call of nature leaves it free. Conversation starts to warm up as the piles of charred pitas arrive along with an array of colourful whipped dips and bowls of glossy olives. Once we are all settled in, a second wave of dishes appears; small plates, some steaming hot, some chilled, all delicious. I hear the music from Zorba the Greek playing in the background (and briefly wonder if it's just in my own head) as the animated conversation around me reaches a crescendo and plate after plate of lovingly made food continues to appear on the table in front of us.

As the bottom of each plate starts to peep through, a waiter discreetly slips it under another full one and another wave of *mezedes* hits the table. This time the scent of the ocean arrives with it: deep-fried calamari, octopus, grilled fish, an aquatic precursor to the meats. Lemons are juggled across the table, pinches of salt scattered across dishes, the concept of eating together is not contrived, it's just the way it is

smell of charcoal, charred lamb and rich stews meanders through the air, making the carnivores salivate as if the previous hours of food hadn't existed. Then the meats arrive, again as before, small dishes, rich in flavour and just enough to share with a little left over. More pitas are ordered, wine glasses are topped up – kids sneak a sip whenever the watchful eyes of the higher-ranking family members wander. Heated debate, that to an outsider might sound like a family intervention, is just the whispering of sweet nothings for us, and I am guessing it's the same for all the other Greek and Cypriot families as well.

There comes a point when the food slows, empty dishes and plates start to disappear from the table and the unconscious hankering for something sweet is satisfied when a selection of bite-sized desserts arrive. *Baklava*, *glyko* – one or two bites is just enough to sate the need for sugar and are washed down with a strong Greek coffee and a shot of *zivania* (a clear Cypriot brandy). So what makes a *meze*? Simply put,

it is small plates, any of your choosing, brought to the table on what appears to be a conveyor belt of food – the only criteria is that you have good company to share it with. The food is, of course, divine, but we all know it's not really about that... it's about the family, the friends, the conversation and the human connections. Philosophizing, making controversial statements designed to raise embarrassed laughter, debating about life, love and the world with a little local gossip thrown in for good measure – you know, all the important stuff in life. To share food is to create a bond and the tradition of breaking bread is as old as time itself with one purpose; to build relationships. So many cultures have their own tradition of small shared plates from Spanish *tapas* and Venetian *cicchetti* to Moroccan *kemia*. Sometimes it is as simple as a small selection of nibbles to be grazing on with a glass of wine at sunset, sometimes it is a substantial feast eaten as a meal, but there are no rules other than to enjoy the food, the company and yourself!

SEA BREAM & WATERMELON CEVICHE
tsipoura me karpouzi ceviche

On hot afternoons in Cyprus, sometimes I'd be quietly lazing about, with only the scent of the sun-kissed earth between the lemon trees and sound of the waves meandering through the air for company... Suddenly I'd hear shouts of 'Karpouzi! Karpouzi!' as a gravelly voiced old farmer drove through the village in an open-top trailer piled high with watermelons. But I didn't mind being startled and falling off my chair... they were damn good watermelons. My ceviche is inspired by those moments and the memory of eating the sweet fruit with the juices running down my chin and the salty breath of the sea.

1 sea bream fillet (120 g/4$^{1}/_{4}$ oz.)
1 garlic clove
freshly squeezed juice of 2 lemons
70 g/2$^{1}/_{2}$ oz. watermelon, flesh diced into 1.25-cm/$^{1}/_{2}$-inch cubes
20 g/$^{3}/_{4}$ oz. red onion, finely diced
1 teaspoon finely diced fresh red chilli/chile
a generous pinch of freshly chopped coriander/cilantro leaves
1 tablespoon olive oil
salt
crisply toasted pita bread, to serve

SERVES 2 AS AN APPETIZER OR 4 AS MEZE

If it isn't already prepared, prepare the fish fillet by skinning and deboning it, and cutting away the darker meat that runs lengthways along the fish where the skin was. The easiest way to do this is, once the fillet is skinned and deboned, simply turn it over (skinned-side up) and cut a 'v' lengthways along the middle. Once done, cut the flesh into 1.25-cm/$^{1}/_{2}$-inch cubes.

Gently crush the garlic clove to just break the shell but keep the clove whole, more or less.

Add the garlic, cubed fish and lemon juice to a bowl, ensuring the fish is completely covered by the lemon juice. Let it 'cook' for 15 minutes, by which time it will have turned opaque.

Remove the fish from the lemon juice, shaking off any excess liquid, and place the fish in a clean bowl (reserving the liquid). Add the watermelon, red onion, chilli and coriander a little at a time, tasting to ensure the flavour is evenly balanced. Once done, add the olive oil, a pinch of salt and a teaspoon of the reserved lemon liquid.

Serve immediately. It goes well with some crisply toasted pita bread.

Tip: You can substitute sea bream with sea bass. Always ensure you use the freshest fish possible.

SALT-BAKED BEETROOT WITH WILD GARLIC
pantzariasalata

One of the mainstays at our family's kitchen table is a bowl of *pantzariasalata*. At its heart, it is sliced beetroot with a light dressing of olive oil, vinegar and raw slices of garlic. Here salt-baking the beetroot both intensifies the flavour and seasons it, while the wild garlic leaves and flowers maintain that traditional flavour combination but in a slightly more subtle way.

1 egg white
350 g/1³/₄ cups coarse rock salt
150 g/³/₄ cup sugar
4–5 small beetroots/beets (about 350 g/12 oz.)
a few sprigs of fresh thyme
1 small garlic clove, peeled
12 wild garlic/ramps leaves
freshly ground black pepper
olive oil, for drizzling
red wine vinegar, for drizzling

a roasting pan or deep-sided baking sheet, lined with baking parchment

SERVES 6

Preheat the oven to 180°C (360°F) Gas 4.

First make the salt crust by whisking the egg white, then folding in the salt and sugar. You should have a wet cement-type consistency; add more salt if needed.

Put a little of the salt mixture in the centre of the parchment on the prepared roasting pan to make a bed for the beetroots to sit on. Group the beetroots together on top of this, add the thyme sprigs and spoon the remaining salt mixture over the top, ensuring the beetroots are fully covered. Bake in the oven for 1¹/₂–2 hours, depending on the size of the beetroots.

Once done, leave to cool for 10 minutes before breaking open the salt crust. Remove the beetroots and, while they are still warm (but cool enough to handle), peel the skin off. If they go cold, the skin is harder to peel. Slice the beetroots into discs about 5 mm/¹/₄ inch thick. (A good life hack is to rub olive oil on your hands before touching the beetroot and it stops it staining your fingers!)

Slice the garlic as thinly as you can scatter it over the beetroot. Season with black pepper and drizzles of olive oil and vinegar. Roughly slice the wild garlic leaves, leaving a few whole just for show, and gently fold all the ingredients together. Serve at room temperature.

Tip: If you have wild garlic flowers you can add these to the salad as a final garnish, dotted over the salad after you have plated up.

RAINBOW TOMATO SALAD
ouranio toxo salada me tomades

There is almost nothing as wonderful and satisfying to eat as a naturally
grown tomato. Bursting with colour, sweetness, and a heady summer
aroma that lingers in the air, a beautiful plump tomato is a gift from the Gods.
Buy tomatoes in season and never store them in your fridge. I always include
a few of the plum variety in this salad to ensure sweetness and then simply
anoint them with a pomegranate molasses and white balsamic dressing to
complement their ripe flesh. Served flat on a plate, rather than elbowing each
other in a bowl, this recipe treats tomatoes with the respect a gift deserves.

**500 g/1 lb. 2 oz. ripe heirloom
tomatoes**
1/4 red onion
**2 tablespoons freshly chopped
flat-leaf parsley**
a pinch of Greek dried oregano
**4 tablespoons white balsamic
vinegar**
1 teaspoon pomegranate molasses
2 tablespoons pomegranate seeds
**sea salt flakes and freshly ground
black pepper**
olive oil, for drizzling

SERVES 8 AS MEZE

Slice the tomatoes about 1.25 cm/1/2 inch thick and gently layer them
in a serving dish. Slice the red onion as finely as you can and scatter over
the tomatoes, followed by the chopped parsley.

Season generously with the oregano and some coarsely ground black
pepper and a pinch of sea salt flakes.

Drizzle over some olive oil, just a couple of shakes to let it seep through
the crevices between the tomatoes.

Mix together the balsamic vinegar and pomegranate molasses to give
you a rich purple dressing (you can up the quantities of this and store for
another day; I love it). Sprinkle some of it over the tomatoes and finish
with a light scattering of pomegranate seeds.

There is nothing more to do. At a push, a few shavings of Kefalotyri
cheese won't hurt it, but tomatoes are very self-conscious and would hate
to feel overdressed.

SALAD FOR THE SOUL
kolifa

This salad is inspired by *kolifa*, a dish served during a *mnimosino* in the Greek Orthodox church. *Mnimosino* is a memorial service for loved ones who have passed. *Kolifa* is a symbolic and decorated dish and (I don't know why I feel guilty about this) it tastes delicious. Whenever I've attended church for one of these services, the family will have made their own version of *kolifa* and, using a tea saucer, scoop out a portion, pop it into a little food bag and hand one to whomever is within reaching distance. I never say no. Paying homage to the headline ingredients of wheat berries, pomegranate seeds, raisins, almonds and sesame seeds, every family makes their own version of this special dish.

160 g/1 cup wheat berries
40 g/¼ cup white quinoa
40 g/¼ cup black quinoa
2 tablespoons sesame seeds
3 spring onions/scallions
¼ red onion
a handful of fresh mint
a handful of fresh flat-leaf parsley
a handful of fresh coriander/ cilantro
seeds of 1 pomegranate
20 g/2 tablespoons (dark) raisins
1 fresh red chilli/chile
a handful of flaked/sliced almonds, toasted
1 lime
salt and freshly ground black pepper
olive oil, for drizzling

SERVES 6–8 AS MEZE

Start off by cooking all of the grains. You cook them all in simmering water, the only difference being the duration. Cook the wheat berries for about 40–50 minutes, until they are soft but still a little chewy – you don't want any crunch to these; their gift is in their chewiness. Cook the black quinoa for about 20 minutes, and cook the white quinoa for about 12 minutes. All in different saucepans.

Once cooked, drain the grains and lay out on a baking sheet to cool and steam dry. Leave the quinoa naked, but dress the wheat berries with a drizzle of olive oil and some seasoning whilst still warm.

Separately, steep the sesame seeds in a little boiling water until you are ready to use them – this just helps to soften them and plump them up.

Finely slice the spring onions, including the green parts, and place in a bowl. Finely dice the red onion and chop all the herbs. Add to the bowl. Cut the pomegranate into quarters and then hold each one and whack the skin side with a wooden spoon (or any fairly large object for that matter) so it kicks out all the seeds. If you get carried away you'll pebble-dash your kitchen in red dots. Add all the seeds to the bowl.

Coarsely chop the raisins, finely chop the chilli (add as much or as little as you prefer), throw in the toasted flaked almonds and season generously, and I mean generously.

Add the cooled grains to the bowl and mix it all together. Give it a good drizzle of olive oil and squeeze in the juice of half a lime, taste, and decide if you want to add the rest.

SEARED GOAT'S CHEESE WITH HAZELNUTS & HONEY
tyri gidas me fintoukia kai meli

The salad on its own is delicious and clean-tasting, but topped with a little warm goat's cheese, preferably one with a rind as it holds its shape better when seared, and dressed in a two-tone drizzle of golden Greek honey and ruby red pomegranate molasses, it's really something special. A welcome little crunch and texture is introduced by the hazelnuts.

1 beetroot/beet
2 garlic cloves
a sprig of fresh thyme
a splash of cider vinegar
6 broccolini spears (such as Tenderstem)
6 fresh asparagus spears
a handful of baby spinach leaves
100 g/3^1/$_2$ oz. goat's cheese log
1 tablespoon Greek honey
1 tablespoon pomegranate molasses
1 tablespoon toasted hazelnuts, sliced
celery salt and cracked black pepper, to taste
olive oil, for cooking and drizzling

SERVES 2 AS MEZE

Preheat the oven to 180°C (360°F) Gas 4.

Drizzle a little olive oil over the beetroot, season, place onto some foil with the whole garlic cloves and the thyme, and wrap to close. Bake in the preheated oven for about 1 hour.

Once the beetroot is cooked, let it cool a little, then peel away the skin and cut it into about eight segments, give or take. Splash it with a little vinegar, add a pinch of celery salt and a drizzle of olive oil.

To prepare the broccolini, cut the spears from the stalk, then blanch in salted boiling water for a minute before dropping into a bowl of iced water or rinse under a very cold running tap. Place on a paper towel to dry.

Leave the asparagus in long spears, just trim any tough stalks away. Combine the asparagus and broccolini. Both need nothing more than a little caress with olive oil and a pinch each of celery salt and pepper. Drop them onto a really hot griddle/grill pan for a couple of minutes, then remove from the pan and place into a mixing bowl. Immediately throw in a handful of baby spinach leaves with the asparagus and broccolini, so the residual heat just wilts the spinach. Decant the beetroot portions into the bowl with the greens (shaking off any excess dressing), season again if needed, and fold through the ingredients, then place onto a serving dish.

Finally, get a non-stick frying pan/skillet really hot. Cut the goat's cheese into 2.5-cm/1-inch thick discs and, when the pan is ready, sear the cheese for a minute before turning it over for 30 seconds. Try not to poke around when the cheese is in the pan, just leave it alone until ready to flip. You should have a nice golden sear to the top of the goat's cheese. Place the cheese on top of the leaves, drizzle over the honey, followed by the pomegranate molasses, and finally scatter the hazelnuts over the top.

ROASTED AUBERGINE DIP
melitzanosalada

Soft, molten aubergine flesh, smoky from roasting, is laced with the subtle heat and flavour of fresh garlic. Drizzle with olive oil, add a sprinkle of chopped parsley and serve with some toasted bread for dipping. I like to serve this at our barbecues as something delicious and simple to share, but always save half of it for when everyone has gone home!

2 aubergines/eggplants, halved lengthways
a few drops of freshly squeezed lemon juice
1 garlic clove, finely crushed
2 tablespoons toasted breadcrumbs
1 tablespoon olive oil, plus extra for drizzling
1 tablespoon finely chopped fresh flat-leaf parsley, plus extra to garnish
salt and freshly ground black pepper

SERVES 6

Preheat the oven to 200°C (400°F) Gas 6.

Place the aubergines onto a baking sheet, drizzle with olive oil and season with salt and pepper, then roast in the preheated oven for 1 hour. Once cooked, leave to cool slightly, then scrape out the flesh. Add the lemon juice and a pinch of salt and pepper, and mash with a fork. Put the mashed aubergine into a sieve/strainer and leave to rest above a bowl for 15–20 minutes, occasionally pressing down with a fork.

Put the aubergine mixture into a bowl and add the garlic, toasted breadcrumbs, olive oil and parsley. Taste for seasoning – it may need a little more salt and pepper, and maybe a tiny bit more lemon, but go easy on the lemon juice as it can take over the delicate flavour of the aubergine.

CHARRED CHILLI & FETA DIP
mavrismene tsilli kai feta voutia

This is one of my favourite dips and is actually inspired by a sauce I tried when travelling through Peru. Blackened fresh jalapeño chillies blended with herbs and feta creates a tangy dip with a real kick. I find it tastes even better the day after it's made and it is great as a marinade for white meat on the barbecue/grill. Serve with lots of crispy toasted pita strips and an ice cold beer.

1 green jalapeño chilli/chile
1 yellow jalapeño chilli/chile
1 small garlic clove
20 g/³/₄ cup fresh coriander/cilantro, including stalks
about 6 fresh mint leaves
60 ml/¹/₄ cup olive oil
a generous pinch of salt
1 teaspoon cider vinegar
1 tablespoon freshly squeezed lemon juice
2 tablespoons Greek yogurt
100 g/3¹/₂ oz. feta cheese

SERVES 6

Preheat the oven to 200°C (400°F) Gas 6.

Either blacken the chillies over an open flame on the gas hob/stovetop – you can thread them onto a long-handled fork to do this – or use a chef's blow torch, if you have one. Place them in a roasting pan and roast in the preheated oven for about 10 minutes.

Remove the stalks from the chillies and drop them whole into the cup of a blender. Add all the other ingredients and whizz. That's it! You are done.

YELLOW SPLIT PEA DIP WITH TOASTED SPICE
fava me frigavismena baharika

This dish has nothing to do with broad (fava) beans. Fava – the dip – is made from yellow split peas puréed into a smooth garlic- and olive oil-laden dip. I add the toasted spices on top – though not traditional, I think it gives a nice textural contrast to the velvety soft purée. I also add a tiny pinch of ground turmeric, to add a subtle earthiness and bring out the lovely sunshine colour.

100 g/½ cup yellow split peas
a pinch of ground turmeric
½ tablespoon coriander seeds
a generous pinch of cumin seeds
a generous pinch of fennel seeds
a generous pinch of black peppercorns
a generous pinch of Szechuan peppercorns
a pinch of dried chilli/hot red pepper flakes
1 garlic clove, crushed
60 ml/¼ cup olive oil, plus extra for drizzling
a few drops of freshly squeezed lemon juice
salt

SERVES 6

Rinse the yellow split peas in cold water a few times, then put them into a pot and add the turmeric and 600 ml/2½ cups water. Bring to the boil and simmer, with a lid on, for about 1 hour. Check towards the end of cooking to make sure the split peas don't dry out.

Meanwhile, dry-fry the whole spices for 1 minute in a frying pan/skillet, then coarsely grind them using a pestle and mortar or spice grinder. Once ground, add the chilli flakes and a pinch of salt. Set aside. What you don't use of this you can save for general seasoning for other meals.

Once the split peas are done, they should be quite mushy with no bite; try a few to check the texture. Drain a little bit of the water into a cup and reserve. You don't need to drain the rest; a little excess cooking liquid is needed to help blend them.

Using a hand-held blender, pulse the split peas until you have a purée, adding some of the reserved liquid from the cup if needed, then blend in the crushed garlic, olive oil, lemon juice and a few really generous pinches of salt (it can take a lot of salt). Blend again until everything is incorporated and smooth, then taste. You may want to add more salt, lemon juice or olive oil, so keep going, taste, and stop when you are happy. Bear in mind this will thicken as it cools to room temperature, so if it is too thick, add a little water just to loosen it.

To dress the fava, spread it onto a plate, scatter the toasted spices over the top and drizzle with extra olive oil just before serving.

SPINACH & FETA BALLS WITH WATERMELON
spanakopita me karpouzi

One of my signature *meze* dishes (you have to eat it with the watermelon), this recipe is inspired by *spanakopita*, a popular flaky filo pastry pie stuffed with spinach and feta.

250 g/9 oz. feta cheese, crumbled
90 g/3¼ oz. watermelon flesh
a pinch of freshly grated nutmeg
200 g/7 oz. fresh spinach, blanched in hot water, drained and squeezed as dry as possible
130 g/1 cup plain/all-purpose flour
2 eggs, whisked with a dash of water
50 g/1 cup fresh breadcrumbs
about 20 fresh mint leaves
freshly ground black pepper
vegetable oil, for frying

MAKES ABOUT 20 BALLS

Put the crumbled feta in a mixing bowl and add the nutmeg and a pinch of ground black pepper. Tip in the spinach and mix thoroughly. Take a small portion and roll into a ball. Repeat with the remaining mixture until you have around 20 small balls. Cut the watermelon into 20 squares, no bigger than the balls and set aside.

Place the flour, egg wash and breadcrumbs into three separate bowls. Dust each ball first in the flour, then in the egg wash, and repeat. Finish with a coating of breadcrumbs and roll gently to help them stay put.

Heat the oil in a deep saucepan until a few breadcrumbs sizzle but take 20–30 seconds to turn golden. Gently place the balls in the hot oil and cook for 2–3 minutes until golden then remove immediately and drain on paper towels. To serve, thread a mint leaf, watermelon square and a ball onto cocktail sticks.

COURGETTE & FETA FRITTERS
kolokitho-keftedes

Clichéd as it is, every Greek household really does make their own version of these. I make mine as I like to eat them and I recommend you do the same. I've added a few toasted pine nuts... because I like them, so there.

85 g/1 cup very finely grated courgette/zucchini (about 1 large courgette)
a pinch of salt
a small pinch of sugar
a generous handful of fresh dill
a handful of fresh flat-leaf parsley
a handful of fresh mint
2 tablespoons plain/all-purpose flour, plus extra for dusting
50 g/1¾ oz. feta cheese
20 g/¾ oz. halloumi cheese
4 tablespoons toasted pine nut kernels
vegetable oil, for frying
Red Pepper & Feta Salsa, to serve (see page 30)

MAKES ABOUT 12 FRITTERS

Place the grated courgette in a bowl and add a pinch of salt and sugar. Mix well and leave in a sieve/strainer set over a bowl for 10 minutes. When you are ready, squeeze as much moisture out of the courgette as possible and then add to a bowl with all the other ingredients. Mix thoroughly. It should hold together enough that you can roll it into 12 neat balls.

Heat the oil in a deep frying pan/skillet over medium heat until a few breadcrumbs sizzle but take 1 minute before turning golden. Dust the balls in flour, then deep-fry for a few minutes until golden. Remove from the oil and drain on paper towels. Serve hot with the salsa on the side.

RED PEPPER & FETA SALSA
peperia kai feta salsa

A classic Greek dip of roasted sweet peppers complementing the tangy feta. I add a fresh tomato to give it a sweet sharpness that I feel brings it all alive, but if you want something a little more sultry, you can use a sun-dried one. Like many dips, this also works really well as a marinade. I'll also admit to adding some store-bought chilli sauce to it and pasting it over fish to roast in the oven.

2 red (bell) peppers, halved, pith and seeds removed
4 garlic cloves, unpeeled
4 sprigs of fresh thyme
4 tablespoons olive oil, plus extra for drizzling
a few drops of freshly squeezed lemon juice
a small pinch of cayenne pepper
1 ripe vine tomato (or 2 baby plum tomatoes)
100 g/3¹/₂ oz. feta cheese, crumbled
1 tablespoon finely chopped fresh flat-leaf parsley
salt and freshly ground black pepper

SERVES 6

Preheat the oven to 200°C (400°F) Gas 6.

Place the pepper halves onto a baking sheet with a garlic clove and sprig of thyme under each one. Drizzle with olive oil, season with a little salt and pepper and roast in the preheated oven for 20–25 minutes, until they start to char.

Squeeze the roasted garlic cloves out of their skins and drop them into the cup of a blender, followed by the roasted peppers, half the olive oil, the lemon juice, cayenne pepper and tomato. Blend to a pulp. Pour out the mixture, add the crumbled feta, the remaining olive oil and the chopped parsley, and fold through.

VEGETABLE TEMPURA
lahanika tempura

Crisply-fried wafer-thin vegetables in a featherlight batter served with a creamy tahini dip and sharp pomegranate molasses.

¹/₂ tablespoon tahini
4 tablespoons Greek yogurt
freshly squeezed juice of 1 lemon
¹/₂ aubergine/eggplant, sliced into long ribbons
1 carrot, sliced very finely lengthways
1 courgette/zucchini, sliced into long ribbons
4 mushrooms, cleaned and stalks removed
4 spring onions/scallions, whole
4 fresh asparagus spears, stalks trimmed

250 ml/1 cup cold tonic water
100 g/1 cup cornflour/ cornstarch
75 g/generous ¹/₂ cup plain/ all-purpose flour
finely chopped fresh flat-leaf parsley
1 teaspoon each of salt and ground pepper
vegetable oil, for deep-frying
pomegranate molasses, for drizzling
fresh dill, to garnish

SERVES 4

To make the dressing, mix the tahini, yogurt and 1 tablespoon of lemon juice together and season with salt and pepper. Set aside.

To make the batter, put the tonic water, cornflour, flour, parsley and 1 teaspoon each of salt and pepper into a bowl and mix with a fork but don't whisk thoroughly – you want it thick and a bit lumpy.

Heat the oil in a stainless-steel frying pan/skillet until a drop of batter sizzles immediately but takes 30 seconds to brown. Working in batches, dip the vegetables into the batter, shake off any excess and fry for about 30 seconds on each side until just starting to turn off-white. Transfer to paper towels with a slotted spoon. Serve hot with the tahini dressing on the side and a drizzle of pomegranate molasses over the top and a little dill to garnish.

GIANT BAKED BEANS IN TOMATO SAUCE
gigantes plaki

'Giant baked beans' are a dish woven into the tapestry of Greek cuisine and have been around for as long as anyone can remember. Like so many Greek dishes, gigantes plaki stem from simple village food using ingredients grown an arms-length away from the kitchen. Slow cooked, these can be eaten warm or at room temperature and go with just about anything.

340 g/2 cups gigante beans (or butter/lima beans), soaked for 24 hours
^{1}/$_2$ onion, diced
1 small carrot, diced
3 garlic cloves
1 tablespoon smoked paprika
1 teaspoon ground cumin
1 teaspoon ground coriander
a generous pinch of Greek dried oregano
125 ml/^{1}/$_2$ cup Retsina wine
250 ml/1 cup passata/strained tomatoes
1 tablespoon tomato purée/paste
a pinch of dried chilli/hot red pepper flakes
a pinch of sugar
a small handful of fresh flat-leaf parsley
500 ml/2 cups water
a small handful of fresh dill
60 ml/^{1}/$_4$ cup olive oil, plus extra for cooking
salt and freshly ground black pepper
crusty bread, to serve

SERVES 6

Preheat the oven to 180°C (360°F) Gas 4.

After soaking the beans overnight, drain and put them in a pan with fresh water. Bring to the boil and simmer for about 2 hours until cooked without any crunch (I usually do this a day or two before).

Heat a little olive oil in a pan, add the diced onion and carrot, and cook gently for about 10 minutes until nice and soft. Add the garlic and let it warm through for a minute before adding the smoked paprika, cumin, coriander and oregano. Stir through to ensure everything is coated and then add the wine. Simmer and reduce by two-thirds.

Now add the cooked beans, passata, tomato purée, dried chilli flakes, sugar, half the parsley and some salt and pepper. Finally, top with the water to ensure the beans are fully covered.

Bring it to a simmer and then pour into a casserole dish and cook in the preheated oven, loosely covered, for about 2 hours. Check periodically to ensure the beans haven't dried out; it should be thick.

Once it's cooked, add the remaining parsley and the dill, and fold through the olive oil. Taste for seasoning and add salt and pepper if necessary, leave to cool to room temperature and enjoy with plenty of crusty bread for mopping up the unctuous sauce.

Tip: At a push, and if your life depended on it, you could use canned beans, you philistine you. The oven cooking time remains the same.

FILLED CRISPY FILO ROLLS
filo dolmades

Sometimes I fancy a little crunch and these hit the spot. Wafer-thin, layers
of baked filo pastry conceal a moist, aromatic meat filling, sweet with dates,
sharp with cranberries, warming and fresh with herbs and spices. These are
perfect eaten freshly cooked, still warm and crisp from the oven.

1 small onion, finely diced
250 g/9 oz. minced/ground lamb
150 g/5$^{1}/_{2}$ oz. minced/ground pork
2 generous pinches of ground
    cinnamon
a generous pinch of smoked
    paprika
a pinch of ground cumin
a small pinch of ground cloves
2 tablespoons sunflower seeds
2 tablespoons diced pitted dates
2 tablespoons dried cranberries
2 tablespoons Greek dried oregano
$^{1}/_{2}$ tablespoon cornflour/
    cornstarch
100 ml/$^{1}/_{3}$ cup cold water
a handful of fresh flat-leaf parsley,
    chopped
a handful of fresh mint, chopped
12 sheets filo/phyllo pastry
    (25 x 15 cm/10 x 6 inches), see
    Tip, right
50 g/3$^{1}/_{2}$ tablespoons butter,
    melted
1 tablespoon fennel seeds
a pinch of dried chilli/hot red
    pepper flakes
salt
olive oil, for cooking
tzatziki, to serve

*a baking sheet, lined with baking
    parchment*

MAKES ABOUT 12 CIGARS

Preheat the oven to 180°C (360°F) Gas 4.

Heat a drizzle of olive oil in a pan, add the onion and fry until soft and
translucent, but don't let it brown. Add the lamb and pork mince, spices,
seeds, dates, cranberries and oregano, and cook until the meat is well
browned and any residual juices have evaporated.

Make a slurry with the cornflour and cold water and pour into the pan.
Heat until the water bubbles – this is just to loosen the mixture slightly;
it will evaporate quickly. Remove from the heat and add the parsley
and mint.

Lay out a sheet of filo in front of you lengthways and lightly brush the
surface with melted butter. Place a couple of tablespoons of the meat
mixture in the middle, about 2.5 cm/1 inch from the bottom. Roll the pastry
over once, then fold over the edges (a stray finger to push the mixture in
from the edge is virtually mandatory) and roll to the end.

You want quite thick, chunky rolls, so make sure you put plenty of filling
in. Once you've given it a full roll, you can trim the end if need be; you don't
want too much pastry. Place seam-side down on the lined baking sheet.
Repeat with the remaining pastry and filling. Lightly butter the top of each
roll and sprinkle fennel seeds, chilli flakes and salt over the top.

Bake in the preheated oven for 10 minutes, or until the outside shell has
crisped and turned slightly golden. These go well with a little tzatziki and
a cold beer.

Tip: Filo pastry is wafer thin and dries out quickly once unwrapped. It is
very needy so give it constant attention... If you ignore it even for just
a few minutes, it will throw a massive strop, dry out, turn brittle and be
impossible to work with! So don't hang around when you start working
with filo. Each time you remove a sheet of it, either roll the rest back up,
or cover with a damp cloth to keep it moist. Basically show it you care.

CAULIFLOWER WITH TAHINI
frigmeno kounoupithy kai tahini

Warmly-spiced, cumin-roasted cauli works well as both a small *meze* plate or as a side with lamb or a roast chicken. Either serve the yogurt, tahini and honey dressing as a dip, or spread it onto a serving platter and top with the cauliflower for a smarter serve.

1 cauliflower, leaves removed
1 tablespoon cumin seeds
1/2 tablespoon ground cumin
a few drops of freshly squeezed lemon juice
60 ml/1/4 cup Greek yogurt
1 tablespoon tahini
1 teaspoon Greek honey
salt and freshly ground black pepper
olive oil, for drizzling

SERVES 6 AS MEZE

Preheat the oven to 200°C (400°F) Gas 6.

Break the cauliflower into florets. Cut the large ones in half lengthways. Drizzle with olive oil, season with salt and pepper and sprinkle over the cumin seeds and about half of the ground cumin to ensure the cauliflower is well coated. Roast in the preheated oven for 20 minutes before removing, then add a squeeze of lemon juice and let it cool slightly.

To make the dressing, simply mix together the yogurt, tahini, the remaining ground cumin and the honey, and lightly season with salt and pepper. Taste, adding more salt or honey as preferred.

Either serve the dip on the side in a small dish or spread it onto a serving dish (I use the back of a spoon to stretch it out), then arrange the cauliflower in the centre. Give it a little drizzle of olive oil, and serve.

SULTRY AUBERGINES
melizana me melases stafiliou

Glossy, deep purple aubergines feature heavily in Greek cuisine and are incredibly versatile. Here they are thinly sliced, then dressed and cooked in a sticky grape molasses, which adds a rich caramel note (see photograph on page 39).

1 large aubergine/eggplant
1 garlic clove, sliced
1 spring onion/scallion, sliced
2 tablespoons grape molasses
a few drops of dark soy sauce
1/2 teaspoon malt vinegar
salt and freshly ground black pepper
olive oil, for cooking
a few fresh coriander/cilantro leaves, to garnish
a pinch of dried chilli/hot red pepper flakes

SERVES 6 AS MEZE

Cut the aubergines in half lengthways, then cut into slices about 1.25 cm/1/2 inch thick.

Heat a frying pan/skillet with a little olive oil over a high heat and fry the aubergine slices for a few minutes on one side until golden. Drizzle just a little more olive oil into the pan and turn them over to cook the other side. After a few minutes, turn the heat down and add the garlic and spring onion, and cook for a few minutes more. Add the grape molasses, 1 tablespoon water, the dark soy and the vinegar. Shake the pan about a bit until the liquid has reduced, then remove from the heat.

Transfer to a plate, spoon over the liquid and garnish with the coriander leaves, dried chilli flakes and add a little seasoning.

GRANDMOTHER'S MEATBALLS
yiayia's keftedes

I vividly remember my Yiayia (grandmother) making these. Standing in front of the cooker, on one side, a chopping board covered in little uncooked meatballs dusted in flour and still surrounded by a subtle white haze hanging about in the air. In front of her, a skillet bubbling away and on the other side, an empty oil-smeared plate that had all too briefly been home to a dozen freshly cooked meatballs, which now reside in several naughty little boys' bellies... *keftedes*, catnip to kids and I've never met one who doesn't love them. Cypriot *keftedes* differ from Greek ones thanks to the inclusion of grated potato. The shot of brandy, I think, was just my Yiayia's preference...

1 potato
1 small onion
1 slice of white bread, soaked
    in whole milk for 30 minutes
500 g/1 lb. 2 oz. minced/ground
    pork
1 garlic clove, crushed
a small handful of fresh flat-leaf
    parsley
a small handful of fresh mint
a generous pinch of paprika
1 egg, whisked
2 tablespoons brandy (Greek,
    naturally!)
salt and freshly ground black
    pepper
plain/all-purpose flour, for dusting
vegetable oil, for frying

TO SERVE
Greek yogurt
a pinch of ground cumin
a simple tomato salad
lemon wedges, for squeezing

MAKES ABOUT 12 MEATBALLS

Start by grating the potato and onion, then squeezing out as much excess liquid as you can. Place into a large mixing bowl. Squeeze the soaked bread out by hand and add to the bowl. Now add all the other ingredients (except the flour and vegetable oil). Don't be afraid to get your hands dirty – massage all the ingredients together until well combined. If you have time, let the mixture rest for 30 minutes.

Heat the oil in a frying pan/skillet until a pinch of flour immediately sizzles. Take a piece of the mixture and roll into a ping pong ball-sized ball. Repeat to make 12 balls. Dredge the balls in flour and then fry them in the hot pan for a few minutes until they are golden all over and cooked through. Remove from the pan and place on paper towels. Sprinkle with a little salt.

Serve hot or cold with Greek yogurt dusted with ground cumin and salt, a tomato salad and some lemon wedges for squeezing over.

SAUTÉED CHICKEN LIVERS WITH SHERRY
sikodakia kotopoulou me krasi

I think chicken livers are hugely underrated. They are cheap, in abundance, delicate in flavour and frankly delicious. This recipe is quite rich in taste, working perfectly as a *meze* or even an appetizer. Sautéing them in Greek sherry or a sweet Greek red wine such as Mavrodaphne complements the iron-rich notes of the liver, and a little kick of citrus offsets the richness in a way that's just right. Serve with a little charred bread and all the sauce.

70 g/^{1}/$_2$ cup plain/all-purpose flour
100 g/3^1/$_2$ oz. chicken livers
250 ml/1 cup whole milk
60 ml/^{1}/$_4$ cup Greek sherry
15 g/1 tablespoon butter
a few drops of freshly squeezed orange juice, plus a pinch of finely grated orange zest
a few drops of freshly squeezed lemon juice, plus a pinch of finely grated lemon zest
a pinch of finely chopped fresh flat-leaf parsley
salt and freshly ground black pepper
olive oil, for cooking
slices of charred bread, to serve

SERVES 2 AS MEZE

Season the flour heavily with salt and pepper.

Cut away any sinew from the chicken livers and rinse them in the milk. Shake off the excess liquid and dust the livers in the seasoned flour.

Heat a drizzle of olive oil in a pan and, when a pinch of flour immediately sizzles, add the chicken livers to the pan and cook on each side for a couple of minutes, depending on their thickness.

Once nice and crisp and a little firm to the touch (don't embarrass them, but you want them slightly blushing inside), remove them from the pan and set aside.

Pour the Greek sherry into the pan and reduce by two-thirds, then remove from the heat. Once it's stopped bubbling, add the butter and mix thoroughly to create a thick glaze. Add a few drops of orange juice and a few drops of lemon juice, and taste; it should be sweet and just slightly offset with the citrus. If it's too thick, add a teaspoon or two of water.

Put the crispy chicken livers back into the pan and coat with the sauce. Plate up and drizzle over any remaining sauce. Season again, lightly scatter over the chopped parsley and orange and lemon zests, and serve with slices of charred bread.

sea

SEA
thalassa

Let me share the memory of a childhood experience that impacted strongly on how I view food today. I can't have been much older than 7 or 8 on what may have looked to any bystander like an innocent family day out on the beach, but that was far from the reality of the situation. Wading up to my waist in the cool of the crystal-clear waters, my feet delicately danced along the rocky sea bed. One hand held in the safety of my dad's hand, the other tightly clutching a lemon. This was no time for play, we were hunting... or as close to what hunting felt like to a young boy in his Superman swimming trunks with goggles strapped to his head.

We circled around in the water, me jumping up onto tippy-toes as each small wave crashed against my chest. My attention was starting to wane, but then, suddenly, amongst the sharp rocks and welcome feet-soothing patches of sand there appeared dozens of black and purple balls covered in spikes. They looked hostile to me, definitely not cuddly playthings and I felt my grip tighten around my dad's fingers. The moment had come. Bending down, my dad delicately picked one up; I was mesmerized. Was it an aquatic hedgehog, a

monster or perhaps an alien that had fallen to earth? I opened my fingers with nervous excitement and he placed the creature in my hand. It moved very slowly across my palm, as if on a thousand pin-sharp stilts, making me squirm and giggle. Next, my dad picked it up and turned it over to reveal its underside and then quickly cut into it with a pocket knife, releasing a murky liquid. He gave it a shake and then looked at me. The dark shell was a striking canvas for the bright orange lines of flesh (later I found out that they are actually sex organs, which would have been way too much information for me at the time!). He's looking at me so I nod in approval. I think he is doing a good job. He's still looking at me. I have no idea what we're both waiting for. The lemon! I forgot the lemon! I immediately offer it up, he cuts into it with the knife, gives it a little squeeze and drizzles some juice over the orange flesh. Then using just our fingers we each scoop out a piece and eat it. Well, at that moment I thought I was basically king of the world. I was blown away, the idea that we'd hunted, found something and eaten it there and then standing waist high in the sea was just

extraordinary to me. I loved it. It is that immediacy, rawness, simplicity and the direct connection with nature that has left an indelible mark on my psyche, and it is something I strive for and gain huge pleasure from experiencing or creating for others to enjoy.

For thousands of years Greek fishermen have harvested their food from the azure sea, taking their brightly painted fishing boats out from the shelter of the islands' harbours to throw their nets into the open waters. The sea is entwined with Greek and Cypriot life and culture. It is as important to the Greeks today as it was c1,500 BC when stone tablets first referenced Poseidon, the Greek god of the sea. The shores of the 6,000 islands scattered across the Aegean and Ionian take up almost half of Greece's 16,000 km coastline, and the Island of Cyprus sits by itself, surrounded by the blue of the Mediterranean. Not surprising then that the colours of the Greek flag are said to symbolize sky and sea. Greece remains the only European country for which the small-scale artisanal fishing sector has a bigger economic impact than the large-scale fisheries and it has the largest fishing fleet in Europe by number of working boats. That said many islanders still just fish just enough to feed their families or sell locally. The variety of fish available in Greek waters, from *kolios* (mackerel) and *lavraki* (seabass) to *kalamari* (squid) and *soupia* (cuttlefish) is reflected in the breadth of recipes and cooking techniques found in the cuisine; from fast flame-grills and deep-fries to slow-cooked stews.

When we talk about provenance of our food, it isn't limited to land, and if you've ever sat at a beach taverna with your feet in the sand and tasted the freshness of octopus pulled from the sea that morning, tenderized on the rocks, deep-fried and presented to you on a plate, you will know what I am talking about. But the philosophy of championing the simplicity of ingredients doesn't have to stop at the water's edge. When you cook at home with the freshest fish and seafood you can source, it still doesn't need too much doing to it. I'm personally loath to add anything that might mask the beauty of good ingredients in my own kitchen. Basically, the message here is that if you have the best ingredients, you really don't need much else. But whatever you do, don't forget the lemon!

SEAFOOD PASTA WITH OUZO
thalassika zimarika me ouzo

Just the thought of seafood and ouzo, and I am sitting in a beach taverna
with my feet in the sand listening to the sound of the waves crashing in the
distance. This is a humble dish – a bit of pasta, a bit of seafood, a bit of ouzo.
But put them together with a little love and an extra dash of this and that,
you'll create a dish worth salivating over. I like this recipe because of its
humble origins, not despite them. It simply capitalizes on great flavours
working together.

300 g/10^{1}/$_{2}$ oz. dried linguine
   pasta
80 ml/^{1}/$_{3}$ cup olive oil, plus extra
   for drizzling
6 garlic cloves, peeled and sliced
12 baby plum tomatoes, halved
   lengthways
a splash of white wine
20 king prawns/jumbo shrimp
12 clams, washed and cleaned
4 small squid, each sliced into 4
50 ml/3^{1}/$_{2}$ tablespoons ouzo
a handful of freshly chopped
   flat-leaf parsley
a pinch of dried chilli/hot red
   pepper flakes
salt and freshly ground black
   pepper

SERVES 4

Cook the pasta in salted boiling water according to the packet instructions
until al dente.

Meanwhile, heat the olive oil in a pan, add the garlic and fry for a couple
of minutes, not letting the garlic change colour. Add the tomatoes and
white wine, and simmer for 5 minutes until the tomatoes have softened
and the wine has reduced.

Add all the seafood, cover with a lid and cook for a few minutes until
the prawns have changed colour and the clams have opened.

Finally, add the ouzo and a few turns of a pepper mill. Simmer for
a couple of minutes to burn off the alcohol, then remove from the heat.

Once the pasta is al dente, drain and add the pasta to the seafood,
including a couple of tablespoons of the cooking water and half the
chopped parsley. Heat the pasta and sauce together for a couple of
minutes, then remove from the heat and rest for a few moments.

Pour the finished pasta onto a large platter, scatter with the chilli flakes,
the remaining chopped parsley, a pinch of salt and a drizzle of olive oil.

Tip: This recipe works terrifically as a quick mid-week meal, cheating
with a ready-to-use pack of mixed seafood. Alternatively, transform this
into something extravagant and sophisticated by adding some seared
scallops, langoustines or any other of your favourite shellfish.

FISHERMAN'S SOUP
kakavia

Kakavia is the name of the pot in which fishermen would cook their unsellable catch. Small fish, simmered down into a rich broth. It always conjures up a vision for me of a couple of old fishermen, wrinkled with age, sun and salty air, sitting back on the boat after a hard night's fishing. A wooden boat gently bobbing away, a dancing reflection in crystal blue waters. Possibly a small glass of ouzo, a little splash making it into the pot for good measure, maybe even a flick of sea water for seasoning as well... Traditionally, all the fish is cooked down, but I like a few chunks, so I cook it a little differently. Feel free to add any other shellfish and white fish you like; I steer away from using oily fish.

1 onion
1 stick/stalk celery
3 garlic cloves, peeled
350 g/12 oz. new potatoes
a generous pinch of Greek dried
  oregano
400 g/14 oz. fresh tomatoes
a handful of freshly chopped
  flat-leaf parsley
a splash of ouzo
400 g/14 oz. clams, washed and
  cleaned
300 g/10 oz. squid
about 750 ml/3 cups chicken or
  vegetable stock
a handful of freshly chopped dill
2 seabass fillets
500 g/1 lb. 2 oz. hake or cod fillet
1 lemon, for squeezing
a pinch of dried chilli/hot red
  pepper flakes
salt and freshly ground black
  pepper
olive oil, for cooking and drizzling
crusty bread, to serve

SERVES 4

Dice the onion and celery, and sweat down in a frying pan/skillet with a little olive oil. Slice the garlic and stir in.

Dice the new potatoes into 1.25-cm/^{1}/$_2$-inch cubes and throw them into the pot along with the oregano and a generous hit of seasoning. Cook this for about 5 minutes while you prepare the tomatoes.

Dice the fresh tomatoes and place into a bowl. Swish around a little with your hands and then drag out the tomatoes leaving the excess liquid and some of the seeds behind. Drop the tomato flesh into the pot along with the parsley. Splash in the ouzo, preferably from the chilled glass from which you are sipping.

Now add the clams and squid, stir well and pour in enough of the stock to cover. Bring this to a gentle simmer and cook for 20 minutes with the lid off to let the stock reduce a little, then add most of the chopped dill.

Cut the seabass fillets into two, giving you four pieces in total, and cut the hake or cod into four equal portions. Place these on top of the soup and push them down a little to submerge them. Season again. Cover loosely with a lid and let these cook for about 5 minutes or until done, then remove from the heat.

Add a little squeeze of lemon, a drizzle of olive oil, a pinch of chilli flakes and a sprinkle of salt if needed, and let the soup rest for 5 minutes. Serve at the table in the pot and allow everyone to ladle their own soup into bowls, garnished with the remaining dill.Provide some big chunks of good bread.

SLOW-COOKED SQUID
kalamari stifado

This particular cephalopod is a creature of extremes; it can be cooked either very fast at high heat or low and slow. Both methods will reward you with a delicious bite and for this recipe low and slow is the only option. The gentle cooking of the squid gives it time to relax and grow tender in an aromatic bath of ingredients, as it soaks up the flavours and melts into the stew. Plenty of crusty bread on the side is essential here, and *pourgouri* works well too.

250 ml/1 cup olive oil
5 onions, sliced
5 garlic cloves, finely chopped
12 black peppercorns, left whole
5-cm/2-inch piece of fresh ginger, peeled and chopped
2 tablespoons fennel seeds, toasted
12 baby plum tomatoes, halved
2 tablespoons tomato purée/paste
a pinch of sugar
500 g/1 lb. 2 oz. squid
1 tablespoon malt vinegar
a couple of pinches of dried chilli/ hot red pepper flakes
250 ml/1 cup white wine
a small handful of freshly chopped flat-leaf parsley
salt and freshly ground black pepper

TO SERVE
Bulgar Wheat & Vermicelli Noodles (see page 113)
crusty bread

SERVES 4

Add all the olive oil to a pan with the sliced onions and cook on a medium heat until the onions start to turn translucent, about 5–10 minutes, but don't let them colour. Once the onions are cooked, add the garlic and stir through, letting it relax into the pan for a couple of minutes.

Season the onions and garlic, and then add all the other ingredients except the parsley. Be careful when adding the wine to hot oil, I usually do this last, using the rest of the ingredients to buffer it a little as it goes into the pan. Bring the pan to a simmer, then reduce the heat to low, cover and let it cook gently for about 45 minutes–1 hour.

By now, all the ingredients will have amalgamated together, the squid will be wonderfully tender and the olive oil will be carrying lots of flavour.

Allow it to rest for a few minutes and then serve, garnishing the top with the chopped parsley.

Serve with a bowl of herb-infused Bulgar Wheat & Vermicelli Noodles (Pourgouri) and some decent bread to soak up the sauce.

Tip: Normally, when buying fish, it is always recommended to buy the freshest you can. Paradoxically, when buying squid or octopus in the UK, I will choose frozen over fresh every time. The process of freezing squid and octopus tenderizes the meat, with the added bonus it is usually cheaper. Make sure you buy big frozen squid, if you use small calamari they will shrink to nothing, buy big and let the slow-cook tenderize the meat.

GRILLED OCTOPUS WITH SQUID INK LENTILS
octapothe kai kalamari mes pye fakes

I remember trying to catch octopus as a kid while in Cyprus. Hunting for octopus (it is a hunt by the way, not a passive pastime like fishing) is an exercise in dexterity, intellect and speed – and it turns out octopuses have those traits in more abundance than ten-year-old Theo had. I never caught one... Whenever you are going to grill, barbecue or fry an octopus, it always starts with a slow braise to tenderize it. Cooking it on a barbecue is wonderful. The raw heat of hot coals combined with the charcoal smokiness is divine. A super-hot grill makes the best alternative, however, which is how we're going to do this one. You'll also need bread, wine and family for this.

1 octopus, about 2 kg/4¹/₂ lb., prepared* (see Note below)
2 dried bay leaves
3 garlic cloves
1 lemon
¹/₂ teaspoon sumac
a generous pinch of finely chopped fresh flat-leaf parsley
200 g/1 cup pre-cooked Puy lentils
¹/₂ teaspoon squid ink
¹/₂ red onion, thinly sliced
1 fresh red chilli/chile, deseeded and finely sliced
salt and freshly ground black pepper
olive oil, for drizzling

SERVES 8–12

* Note: Rinse the octopus and cut the hood from the body (just above the eyes). Cut just below the eyes to remove the tentacles, keeping them intact (discard the piece holding the eyes). Finally, push the beak from the centre of where the tentacles join.

Place the prepared octopus in a large pot with a few generous pinches of salt, the bay leaves and 2 of the garlic cloves. Cover with enough cold water to cover fully. Bring to a simmer and cook gently for about 45 minutes, until you can pierce the flesh with a knife with little resistance. Don't overcook it, as the suckers on the tentacles will start to come off. Octopus has a habit of floating, so either place a lid on the pot or place a small saucer on top of the octopus to help keep it submerged.

Put the cooked octopus into a bowl with a few glugs of olive oil to stop it sticking. Peel a few strips of rind from the lemon and add to the bowl. Set this one side until ready to cook.

Meanwhile, mash the last garlic clove to a pulp with a little salt. Whisk with a few glugs of olive oil and squeeze in about half the amount of lemon juice to oil. Add the sumac and finely chopped parsley and mix.

Mix the Puy lentils with the squid ink and season with a little pepper. When you are ready to grill/broil the octopus, separate the tentacles with a sharp knife and slice the hood into four pieces. Get the grill/broiler as hot as possible. Shake off the excess olive oil from the octopus, season with a pinch of salt, and then grill/broil it close to the heat for a few minutes until it crisps up. Turn the pieces over and char the other side. Remove and brush over the garlic-lemon-sumac dressing.

Scatter the squid ink Puy lentils over a large platter dish, distribute the sliced red onion amongst the lentils, then randomly place the octopus over the top. Taste for seasoning and finish with a little sliced red chilli.

TRIO OF FRIED SEAFOOD
tria triganida

Tiganida (pron. de-ga-ni-da) loosely means 'to fry', and this trio of fried fish recipes is my nostalgic tribute to days spent on the beach in Cyprus. The crispy outer shell, the soft seafood hiding inside, a sprinkle of salt, a squeeze of lemon, a sea breeze and the hazel eyes of my wife to flirt into – I am a happy man. (Note: my wife, if asked, may state that while writing this I asked what colour her eyes are. I deny this fully.) These are meant as picky pieces to share informally amongst friends. All three recipes are wonderful with just a squeeze of lemon, but if you have the time my Saffron Aioli (see page 67) or Charred Chilli & Feta Dip (see page 24) are great accompaniments (and if you don't have the time, a splash of chilli sauce mixed into a few dollops of mayo is a great alternative!).

For a really crispy and light coating I have used the same dusting recipe for years; half cornflour and half plain flour plus a pinch of seasoning. Don't hesitate to get liberal when seasoning the flour, much like my fried mussels recipe where we heavily season the flour instead of the mussels before cooking (which incidentally, is a recipe I've stolen from my Dad who would cook these during our nocturnal philosophizing sessions that always seemed to end up in the kitchen).

CRISPY CHILLI CALAMARI
kalamari tragano me tsilli

The ubiquitous deep-fried calamari, enjoyed all over the Aegean, needs just a light dusting of flour and brief cooking. Using fresh ingredients is at the heart of most of my recipes, but when it comes to our slippery cephalopods, I prefer to buy previously frozen as the process helps tenderize them.

65 g/¹/₂ cup plain/all-purpose flour
25 g/¹/₄ cup cornflour/cornstarch
1 tablespoon chilli/chili powder
400 g/14 oz. squid, including tentacles, cleaned
1 egg, beaten with a dash of water
salt and freshly ground black pepper
vegetable oil, for frying
a small handful of flat-leaf parsley, to serve
freshly squeezed lemon juice, to serve

SERVES 4

Put the flour, cornflour, chilli powder and some salt and pepper in a ziplock bag and shake it.

Cut the squid into thick rings, 2.5 cm/1 inch wide. Dip into the egg wash, shake off the excess and pop them into the flour mixture. Give it a good shake, ensuring the squid is well coated and ensuring the bag is closed; you won't make that mistake twice...

Heat the vegetable oil in a deep pan until a pinch of flour immediately sizzles but doesn't burn. Drop the calamari into the oil and deep-fry for just 1 minute. Drain on paper towels, season immediately and serve with a little parsley over the top and a few drops of lemon juice.

TURMERIC MUSSELS
kourkoumi mydia

Fried mussels are a delight, especially with a crispy coating and in my view a hint of turmeric. You can cook live mussels and then remove the meat from their shells, or use pre-shelled cooked mussels. I won't lie, I use the latter for pure convenience.

65 g/^{1}/$_2$ cup plain/all-purpose flour
25 g/^{1}/$_4$ cup cornflour/cornstarch
^{1}/$_2$ tablespoon ground turmeric
a pinch of cayenne pepper
400 g/14 oz. shelled mussels
a pinch of dried chilli/hot red pepper flakes
salt and freshly ground black pepper
vegetable oil, for frying
a small handful of coriander/cilantro, to serve
freshly squeezed lime juice, to serve
cocktail sticks/toothpicks

SERVES 4

Put the flour, cornflour, turmeric, cayenne and salt and pepper in a ziplock bag and shake it.

Dab the mussels with paper towels to remove some of their moisture. Toss them in the flour mixture.

Pour enough vegetable oil into a frying pan/skillet to just cover the base. Once the oil is hot, drop the coated mussels into the pan. Don't move them, just let them shallow-fry for a few minutes before turning them over for another couple of minutes. If need be, do this in batches to avoid crowding.

Drain on paper towels, season immediately with salt and a pinch of dried chilli flakes. Serve with a little chopped coriander over the top, a squeeze of lime juice and a bunch of cocktail sticks to eat them with.

LEMON & THYME WHITEBAIT
lemoni kai thymari maritha

Deep-fried whitebait is a speciality of many a Greek restaurant. They should be light and delicate, with just a whiff of dusting to give them a crispy golden armour. Have plenty of lemons on hand for squeezing and don't be a wimp, just eat the whole thing!

65 g/^{1}/$_2$ cup plain/all-purpose flour
25 g/^{1}/$_4$ cup cornflour/cornstarch
a few sprigs of fresh thyme
400 g/14 oz. fresh whitebait
salt and freshly ground black pepper
vegetable oil, for frying
freshly squeezed lemon juice and grated zest,
   to serve

SERVES 4

Put the flour, cornflour and some salt and pepper in a ziplock bag and shake it.

Strip the leaves from the sprigs of thyme and scatter over the whitebait, saving a pinch to garnish. Once you've helped the miniscule thyme leaves weave their way through the whitebait, dust the little slivers of silvery fish in the flour mixture.

Heat the vegetable oil in a deep pan until a pinch of flour immediately sizzles but doesn't burn. Deep-fry the whitebait for a few minutes until they start to turn golden, then drain on paper towels and season with a pinch of salt, pepper and the scattr over the remaining thyme leaves.

These need nothing more than a few grates of lemon zest, a little squeeze of lemon juice and of course, a glass of chilled dry white wine.

SMOKY RED MULLET & WHITE BEAN STEW
marpouni kapnistiko me thalassika fasolia

Red mullet, when responsibly sourced, doesn't receive the accolades it deserves. A beautiful, meaty white fish with a slight sweetness, it works equally well just thrown on the barbecue or outdoor grill or cooked over heat in a pan. This recipe complements the red mullet with a smoky, citrusy white bean base dotted with shellfish.

1/2 onion, chopped
30 g/1/4 cup finely chopped carrot
30 g/1/4 cup finely chopped celery
3 garlic cloves, 2 roughly chopped
   and 1 thinly sliced
720 g/4 cups drained canned
   cannellini beans (3 x 400-g/
   14-oz cans)
125 ml/1/2 cup white wine
1 tablespoon tomato purée/paste
about 1 litre/quart light chicken
   stock
2 dried bay leaves
1/2 tablespoon smoked paprika
a handful of live clams, cleaned
a handful of king prawns/jumbo
   shrimp
a small handful of freshly chopped
   flat-leaf parsley
freshly squeezed juice of 1 lemon
8 small red mullet fillets
   (or 4 large)
1 tablespoon plain/all-purpose
   flour
a small knob/pat of butter
8 scallops, shelled
olive oil, for cooking and
   drizzling
bread, to serve

SERVES 4

Fry the onion, carrot and celery in a little olive oil for a few minutes, then add the 2 cloves of roughly chopped garlic and continue cooking. Add one-third of the cannellini beans, followed by the white wine and tomato purée.

Reduce the wine until almost evaporated, and then add half the stock. Loosely cover the pan and cook on a medium-high heat for 5 minutes.

Remove the pan from the heat and either mash by hand or give it a blitz with a hand-held blender. Pass the mixture through a sieve/strainer and set aside.

In a clean pan, drizzle a little olive oil and very gently fry the clove of thinly sliced garlic, ensuring you don't brown it, then add the bay leaves, smoked paprika and strained paste, and return to the heat.

Add the remaining cannellini beans and enough of the stock to reach a creamy consistency. Simmer this uncovered for 20 minutes until the beans are soft, adding more stock if it starts becoming too thick.

5 minutes before the end, throw in the clams and prawns and cook until the prawns are pink and the clams have opened. Add the chopped parsley and give it a good squeeze of lemon juice.

When you are ready to serve, dust the skin side of the red mullet fillets in a little flour and fry in a little olive oil in a separate pan for a few minutes, before turning over for another minute. Remove from the pan and give the pan a wipe with a paper towel. Add the butter and sear the scallops for 30 seconds on each side, depending on how big they are, then spoon some of the butter over them and remove.

Arrange the white bean and shellfish mixture on a serving plate and place the scallops amongst the beans. Top with the red mullet, flesh-side down and serve warm with plenty of decent bread.

PRAWNS BAKED IN FETA & TOMATO SAUCE
garitha saganaki

Saganaki can take various forms, but all are ultimately cooked in a 'saganaki', a two-handled skillet, be it feta, mussels, *Kefalotyri* cheese or, in this case, prawns. I like my prawn saganaki to be tactile and messy, peeling away shells, licking fingers, dipping bread in the sauce and leaving wine glasses smeared with fingerprints like a crime scene. Keep this informal – it's more fun.

600 g/1 lb. 5 oz. large king prawns/
    jumbo shrimp, shells on
1/2 onion
1 stick/stalk celery
1 garlic clove, crushed
60 ml/1/4 cup white wine
1/2 tablespoon smoked paprika
a generous pinch of Greek dried
    oregano
a pinch of sugar
a generous pinch of dried chilli/
    hot red pepper flakes
a small handful of freshly chopped
    flat-leaf parsley
a small handful of freshly chopped
    dill
2 dried bay leaves
1 tablespoon cider vinegar
1 tablespoon tomato purée/paste
250 ml/1 cup passata/strained
    tomatoes
80 g/3 oz. feta cheese, crumbled
salt and freshly ground black
    pepper
olive oil, for cooking and drizzling
bread, to serve

SERVES 4

Preheat the oven to 180°C (360°F) Gas 4.

Season the prawns and sear them in a little olive oil in a pan set over a high heat until they turn pink, then remove them from the pan – you don't need to cook them through, this just helps coax maximum flavour out of our little pink crustaceans.

Dice the onion and celery. Using the same pan, fry them in a little olive oil until the vegetables soften but don't colour, about 5 minutes. Add the garlic and warm through for just a minute before adding the white wine. Reduce the wine by half, then add the smoked paprika, oregano, sugar, half the chilli flakes, most of the parsley (saving a generous pinch), most of the dill (again save a pinch to garnish), the bay leaves, vinegar, tomato purée and passata.

Season generously with salt and pepper, add a splash of water and simmer on a low heat, so it is lightly bubbling, for about 10 minutes. Add a splash of cold water if it starts to dry out. Reintroduce the prawns to the sauce and pop into the preheated oven for 20 minutes.

Once done, remove from the oven and, while still hot, sprinkle over the crumbled feta, remaining chopped parsley, dill and chilli flakes. Add an extra drizzle of olive oil and serve with plenty of bread to soak up the sauce.

HAKE 'EN PAPILLOTE'
WITH FENNEL & PRESERVED LEMONS
pakaliaros tiligmenos me maratho
kai diatirimena lemonia

Cooking *en papillote* is a great way to cook fish as steaming it inside a paper parcel keeps it moist. I like to prepare my little 'parcels of food love' in baking parchment tied up with string, so once brought to the table, diners can unwrap and reveal their very own surprise dish. This is a meal in itself, but you can make it more substantial by adding a handful of fresh gnocchi underneath the fish which will cook at the same time. This is a useful recipe for entertaining as you can prepare the parcels a few hours in advance, keep them chilled, then just pop them in a hot oven when you are ready to serve.

24 baby spinach leaves, destalked
1 small fennel bulb, thinly sliced
12 fine beans, stalk ends trimmed
2 preserved lemons, sliced
8 baby plum tomatoes, halved
2 garlic cloves, finely chopped
2 hake fillets (250 g/9 oz.)
2 tablespoon freshly chopped dill
a few splashes of white wine
2 small knobs/pats of butter
2 pinches of dried chilli/hot red
   pepper flakes
a few generous pinches of freshly
   chopped flat-leaf parsley
a few generous pinches of freshly
   chopped coriander/cilantro
salt and freshly ground black
   pepper
olive oil, for drizzling
bread, to serve

two 45 x 45-cm/18 x 18-inch
   squares of baking parchment
two 30-cm/12-inch lengths of
   butcher's string/twine

SERVES 2

Preheat the oven to 200°C (400°F) Gas 6.

Lay both the baking parchment squares on a flat surface and drizzle a tablespoon of olive oil in the centre of each piece.

Keeping to a size not much larger than each of the hake fillets, layer half the spinach, fennel, fine beans, about half of the preserved lemon slices and the tomatoes on each baking parchment square. Scatter the garlic over the vegetables, letting it fall through the gaps. Season with salt and pepper. (Don't worry if the vegetables fall about the sides a little.)

Season the hake fillets all over before coating the top of each one in the chopped dill. Place each fillet on top of a pile of vegetables. Splash a little white wine over the top of each one and add a drizzle of olive oil and a small knob of butter. Finally, add half of the remaining preserved lemon to each portion.

Now wrap up your parcels. Place your hands under the overhanging baking parchment and bring together above the ingredients. Tie the string/twine around the top like a shoelace.

Place the parcels on a baking sheet and cook in the preheated oven for 20 minutes (or 25 minutes if the hake fillets are quite thick).

Once cooked, place each parcel on a plate and open it up by simply pulling the string/twine. Ta-da! Serve with nothing more than good bread.

COD WRAPPED IN KADAYIF PASTRY WITH SAFFRON AIOLI
gados tiligmeno me kadeifi kai safra aioli

I originally created this recipe for the opening night of my first Greek pop-up restaurant a few years back. It was part of an elaborate 'ocean bowl' course, of which my favourite bit was this fish wrapped in *kadayif* pastry. This creates a very light crispy coating which complements the fish beautifully. It goes very nicely with a little homemade saffron aioli and, at a stretch, a few fried potato off-cuts dusted in a little salt, pepper and dried oregano. Do try to get a whole cod loin, which is nice and thick and tubular in shape.

600-g/1 lb. 5-oz. cod loin
1 tablespoon paprika
200 g/7 oz. kadayif pastry
1 egg, whisked with a dash of
    water
salt and freshly ground black
    pepper
vegetable oil, for frying

SAFFRON AIOLI
a few strands of saffron
1/2 tablespoon hot water
2 egg yolks
2 teaspoons freshly squeezed
    lemon juice
1 teaspoon crushed garlic
100–150 ml/1/3–2/3 cup light olive
    oil (I find a light oil gives
    a better flavour here as some
    oils can overpower)

SERVES 4

First make the saffron aioli. Crush the saffron strands between your fingertips, put them in a bowl with the hot water and leave to steep. In a clean mixing bowl, whisk together the egg yolks, lemon juice, garlic and a little salt. Slowly pour in the olive oil in a thin stream, whisking all the time. Very quickly it will emulsify. Keep whisking in the olive oil until you have the right consistency. Whisk in the saffron liquid and taste for seasoning. Cover and set aside.

Preheat the oven to 180°C (360°F) Gas 4.

Cut the cod loin into four equal portions and season heavily with salt, pepper and the paprika.

Kadayif pastry dries out fast becoming brittle to work with, so work quickly. Lay out strands of kadayif pastry the same width as each portion of fish and about 20 cm/8 inches long. You want them to be evenly spread.

Dip a piece of fish into the egg wash, shake off the excess, then place at the top of the pastry and roll the pastry around the fish. You want this quite tight and even, with all the strands going in the same direction. Once rolled, lay the fish on a plate, seam-side down. Repeat with the other fish portions and pastry. (You can do up to this bit up to a day in advance.)

Heat the oil in a deep frying pan/skillet until a piece of pastry sizzles immediately but takes 1 minute to brown. Deep-fry each parcel for about 5 minutes until the pastry is hard and has just started to turn golden. Transfer to a wire rack set over a roasting pan and cook in the preheated oven for 5 minutes. If you don't put the fish on a rack, the bottom will go soggy – and nobody wants that! Salt the fish and serve hot with the aioli.

SEAFOOD ORZO RISOTTO
thalassika me kritharaki

At the heart of this dish lies *kritharaki* , a side dish of orzo simmered with tomatoes, and a staple on our Cypriot table. I had it as a kid and now, a generation later, I frequently make the same to satisfy the growing appetites of my own gorgeous sprogs, Eva, Alexi and Luca. I dedicate this recipe to these three, who literally inhale seafood at every opportunity and have also become my most vocal critics. My seafood orzo risotto is the dish I use when I need to win them back over for better reviews... In saying that, I don't mean to imply that this is a kid's dish as it's perfect for all generations and any occasion. At home, I pour the lot onto a big platter for everyone to help themselves.

1 onion, diced
4 garlic cloves, sliced
360 g/2 cups orzo pasta
1/2 teaspoon smoked paprika
160 g/1 cup diced tomatoes
125 ml/1/2 cup white wine
a pinch of saffron threads
about 2 litres/quarts chicken stock
a small handful of finely chopped
    fresh flat-leaf parsley
a pinch of dried chilli/hot red
    pepper flakes
a pinch of fennel seeds
200 g/1 cup sliced squid
a couple of handfuls of live
    mussels or clams, cleaned
a couple of handfuls of prawns/
    shrimp
400 g/14 oz. firm white fish fillets,
    such as cod or monkfish, cubed
75 g/1/2 cup petit pois
a splash of ouzo
freshly squeezed juice of 1 lemon
salt and freshly ground black
    pepper
olive oil, for cooking and drizzling

SERVES 4

In a large, deep-sided frying pan/skillet, fry the onion in a little olive oil for 5–10 minutes until soft but not coloured. Add half the garlic, the orzo and smoked paprika. Fry the orzo for a couple of minutes before introducing the tomatoes, wine and saffron to the pan.

Reduce the wine until almost gone, season, then add half the stock. Simmer gently, giving it an occasional stir, until the stock is absorbed. Add the rest of the stock in batches until the orzo is cooked through, but has a tiny bit of chewiness; this will take around 20–30 minutes. You may need a little less or more stock depending on the size of your orzo. It will thicken as it cools, so keep some stock by in case you need to loosen it later.

Once the orzo is done to your liking, remove it from the heat. Add most of the chopped parsley and the chilli flakes and let it rest. (At this stage, you already have a simple kritharaki that makes a perfect side dish.)

Next, add a little olive oil to a clean pan, add the fennel seeds and the remaining garlic to warm through. Introduce the shellfish and fish to the pan and fry for 1 minute. Add the petit pois and a tablespoon or two of water and cover to cook the seafood for just a few minutes. Remove the lid and let any residual water evaporate, discarding any mussels that do not open. Add a splash of ouzo and reduce until almost gone. Remove from the heat and pour the entire contents into the cooked orzo and fold through.

Add a little more stock if it's too thick. Taste for seasoning, pour onto a large platter, scatter with the remaining chopped parsley, a drizzle of olive oil and a small squeeze of lemon juice.

land

LAND
gi

It's Sunday at my Yiayia's North London home, the epicentre of our family. The proposed start time was about 1 pm, that meant people would arrive at 2 pm the earliest, most likely 3 pm. It's just before 4 pm when we all knock on the door. It swings open blasting an assault on all our senses; the heat is a warm current carrying with it the perfume of many hours spent in the kitchen. A scent of roasting meats, warm spices and sharp herbs and steam escaping from the eruption of vegetables boiling in pots on the stovetop. This is quickly followed by more hot air, only this time of the verbal kind... The cacophony of voices inside suggest hundreds of people have congregated, or perhaps it's just a handful of Greeks. And my family, in particular.

Next comes the physical assault, the surge of hugging arms and multiple kisses being planted on cheeks. For any non-Greeks reading this, if there is one piece of advice I can give on entering a Greek household for a meal, it is this; kiss everyone. I mean everyone. Young, old, male, female, hell, if the dog is cute enough throw one his way as well. Everyone then meanders around the house but will group predominantly in the lounge, not the kitchen, and with good reason. The kitchen is now the designated work area and everyone knows that if you enter Yiayia's domain during this time you'll be put straight to work. So we keep well out of the way. A few disciples sacrifice their day and enter, never to be seen again, or at least until dinner is served. Eventually the vocal gong is rung and we are herded towards the dining table. Unconsciously approaching and positioning ourselves in our usual spots, the dance of dinner commences; the melody and

steps remain constant, it's only the dancefloor that differs from home to home. Children misbehaving, parents disciplining and grandparents calmly surveying the carnage they have unwittingly wreaked on the rest of the world. It's noisy, three generations vying for airtime. Eventually everyone is seated, the food starts to appear and then everyone looks towards one seat, and at the wide-eyed person sitting there, a stranger. There is a guest. An unknown quantity. Fresh meat personified.

Every now and again such a guest would join us at my Yiayia's house. Be it the recently-widowed lady from across the street, an old friend of my uncle's who is in the country for a few days, or just a lost soul from someone's workplace who didn't have anything to do that Sunday. True to the spirit of Greek hospitality they are welcomed with open arms, fed, watered, closely questioned and generally brought into the fold with a take-us or leave-us attitude that I've always felt is more hospitable than simply being polite. This notion of having 'guests' most likely stems from the traditional celebratory feast of Greek Easter and I

suspect the guests we had join us periodically were a sentiment from the past brought into our modern homes. Easter is a hugely important religious date in the Greek Orthodox calendar. The period of lent before Easter is a time for fasting, traditionally excluding all meat and dairy, so Easter Sunday is a day of feasting. Traditionally in Cyprus this would be a whole lamb cooked on a spit in the village. This didn't happen much in North London but a feast was had nonetheless, and it was always a time for families and friends to congregate, along with any strangers we had managed to wrangle. I recall one year in particular, the food was being brought to the table (I say brought, my Yiayia had one of those kitchen hatches, a hole in the wall linking the kitchen to the dining room, a sort of domestic pass). An entire ensemble of different meats had started to appear – we like to have ours like our wine, a good red and white – this time it was chicken and lamb. I noticed that our guest was looking decidedly uneasy so I leant over to my Yiayia and whispered 'I think she's a vegetarian'. Yiayia nodded back at me

confidently, and proudly replied 'it's ho-kay! I've done lamb.'...

I should emphasize that Greek cuisine is not meat-centric, in fact it's the reverse. The staple diet of traditional Greek food is heavy with fish, fruit, vegetables, grains and pulses and extremely healthy. Meat is usually eaten in moderation, and more often than not saved for special occasions, and always thoroughly enjoyed. Greek cuisine, like many other cultures is born out of its environment and terrain. It's no surprise that lamb, goat and game (such as rabbit) are staple meats in Cyprus: hardy short-legged beasts are much more adept at roaming the jagged mountains than cows would be, but saying that, beef and pork are eaten; never decline a rich cinnamon-scented *Stifado* (see page 81) or red-wine-rich *Afelia* (see page 86) when it's on offer. The variety of meat dishes cooked varies quite dramatically from the street-food simplicity of pork or chicken *Souvlaki* (see pages 150–151) to the traditional slow-cooked kid goat *Kleftiko* (see page 83), but all of them are delicious.

LAMB SIRLOIN WITH CUMIN CRUST
arni fileto me kimino

The cumin crust gives a really nice warmth to the lamb and a bit of crunch.
I tend to make more crust mixture than I need and store it in a screwtop jar so
that it can be sprinkled on anything else that takes my fancy, which turns out
to be quite a lot as it happens! Lamb sirloin is a cheaper cut than the cannon,
but it has great flavour and is wonderfully tender and what I use here.

1 tablespoon cumin seeds
$^1/_2$ tablespoon coriander seeds
$^1/_2$ teaspoon fennel seeds
$^1/_2$ teaspoon black peppercorns
a pinch of sugar
a pinch of dried chilli/hot red
   pepper flakes
finely grated zest of 1 small lemon
2 pinches of Greek dried oregano
500 g/1 lb. 2 oz. sirloin lamb
salt and freshly ground black
   pepper
olive oil, for drizzling

TO SERVE (optional)
Whipped Garlic Potatoes (see page
   142)
Feta & Mint Greens (see page 102)
Cauliflower with Tahini (see page
   37)

SERVES 2–4

Preheat the oven to 200°C (400°F) Gas 6.

Toast the cumin seeds, coriander seeds, fennel seeds and peppercorns
in a dry frying pan/skillet for a couple of minutes until they release their
aroma, then remove from the heat. Using a pestle and mortar or spice
grinder, grind the toasted spices to a coarse grain, then combine with the
sugar, dried chilli flakes, lemon zest and oregano. Store in an airtight jar.

The sirloin of lamb is a beautiful cut of meat and needs very little
manhandling to get the best from it. At most, score the top of the lamb,
the skin side, to stop it curling in the pan. Season the lamb all over with
salt and pepper, and then place skin-side down in a hot ovenproo pan and
fry for 5 minutes without touching. I mean it, don't touch it.

After 5 minutes, flip it over, generously cover the top (the side you
scored) with the crust mixture, pat it down a little, then transfer to the
preheated oven and roast for 6 minutes. Take it out and let it rest for
10 minutes before carving into thick strips at an angle.

Serve with sides of Whipped Garlic Potatoes, Feta & Mint Greens and
Cauliflower with Tahini for a substantial meal.

Tip: You can add small pile of the crust mixture on the side of each
serving plate for sprinkling.

CYPRIOT LAMB SHANKS IN STICKY SAUCE
arni kormou tis kyprou

This was one of the first recipes I cooked for us to bring a little Greek culture to an East London flat. I remember cooking this years ago when my then girlfriend, now wife, and I moved in together in Canning Town in London (I'm sure she was doing a try-before-you-buy strategy on me… luckily for me, the returns policy has now expired).

4 lamb shanks
2 onions, sliced
4 garlic cloves, chopped
1 tablespoon smoked paprika
$^1/_2$ tablespoon ground cumin
$^1/_2$ tablespoon ground coriander
$^1/_2$ tablespoon ground cinnamon
a pinch of cayenne pepper
1 cinnamon stick
$^1/_2$ teaspoon ground cloves
    or 5 whole cloves
250 ml/1 cup red wine
3 tablespoons pomegranate
    molasses
1 tablespoon Greek honey
3 dried bay leaves
100 g/$^3/_4$ cup pitted ready-to-eat
    prunes (or apricots)
500 ml/2 cups passata/strained
    tomatoes
salt and freshly ground black
    pepper
olive oil, for cooking
2 tablespoons toasted pistachio
    nuts, chopped, to garnish
a generous pinch of dried rose
    petals (see Tip on p.165),
    to garnish
freshly chopped coriander/cilantro,
    to garnish (optional)

SERVES 4

Preheat the oven to 180°C (360°F) Gas 4.

Season the lamb shanks generously and brown them in hot olive oil in a lidded ovenproof pan until coloured all over, then remove from the pan and set aside.

In the same pan, fry the onions slowly for about 10 minutes until they have coloured and turned a deep golden hue, then add the garlic and cook for a few more minutes.

Add all the spices and stir through to coat the onions, then add the wine. Cook with a lide and cook over a high heat to reduce the wine by half. This will concentrate the flavour of the sauce.

Finally, add all the other ingredients and return the lamb shanks to the pan, bottom-side down, so the bone is sticking up. Slowly add about 500 ml/2 cups of water, just enough to cover the meat (the bones can stick out). Bring this to a simmer, then cover and place in the preheated oven for 2 hours.

Once done, remove the pan from the oven and let it rest for 10 minutes before removing the lid.

Serve the lamb shanks sitting upright, with a few ladles of the juice poured over. Garnish with the pistachios and rose petals, as well as some freshly chopped coriander, if you like.

CYPRIOT ROASTED LAMB CHUNKS & POTATOES
arni tava

My Yiayia, Sophia, used to make lamb *tava* back in her village in Cyprus when my mother was just a little girl. She would prepare it at home on a Sunday morning and then take it to the village *fourno* (a communal oven shared by the villagers) on the way to church. After the service, they would all walk back to the fourno and pick up their Sunday dinner, which would then be served with a simple green salad. I haven't altered that family recipe very much at all, but this isn't really about following a specific recipe... it is about instinct and using what is available, and I love it for that. I've used a lamb shoulder, which is how we do it, but you can easily replace the lamb with a couple of small chickens.

1 kg/2¼ lb. lamb shoulder, cut into chunks on the bone
500 g/1 lb. 2 oz. Cyprus potatoes
1 onion
6 garlic cloves, unpeeled
3 small preserved lemons
a pinch of chilli/chili powder
a pinch of ground cinnamon
a small handful of Greek dried oregano
2 tablespoons dried mint
a few sprigs of fresh rosemary or thyme
3 dried bay leaves
2 cinnamon sticks, broken
1 tablespoon tomato purée/paste
freshly squeezed juice of 1 lemon, plus extra to serve
3 large tomatoes
salt and freshly ground black pepper
olive oil, for drizzling
a small handful of freshly chopped flat-leaf parsley, to garnish (optional)

SERVES 6

Preheat the oven to 160°C (325°F) Gas 3.

Ask your butcher to cut the lamb shoulder into small, on-the-bone chunks (about half the size of a fist), trim off any excess fat and add to a large roasting pan.

Peel and quarter lengthways the potatoes. Slice the onion, lightly crush the garlic cloves (leaving the skin on) and slice the preserved lemons into quarters. Mix the lot into the roasting pan with the lamb.

Season generously with salt and pepper. Add the chilli powder, ground cinnamon, oregano, mint, rosemary or thyme (whichever you have available), bay leaves, broken cinnamon sticks and tomato purée.

Squeeze the lemon juice into the mixture. Cut the squeezed lemon into half a dozen chunks and drop them into the pan as well. Mix everything up a little with your hands. Finally, slice the tomatoes into about eight segments and dot over the top, followed by a generous drizzle of olive oil. Give the whole pan a final shake.

Cover tightly with foil and roast in the preheated oven for 1 hour, then remove the foil and roast for a further hour or until the meat starts to char. Remove from the oven, cover loosely with foil and let it rest for 10 minutes before serving. You can garnish with a little fresh parsley, if you like, and an extra squeeze of lemon.

Note: If your lamb shoulder chunks are quite large, you can roast it while covered for another 30 minutes without any problems.

BRAISED BEEF SHORT RIBS WITH ONIONS
vothino stifado me mikro-paithaki

Stifado is one of Greek cuisine's most famous dishes. Slow-cooked, sweet and soft baby onions are lovingly wrapped in a blanket of rich, aromatic sauce and usually found cuddling up to chunks of beef, rabbit or even octopus. My version pays homage to the true foundations of *stifado*, but fuses it with mouth-wateringly tender beef short ribs for a crowd-pleasingly modern take.

1 kg/2¼ lb. baby onions
4 meaty beef short ribs
(about 1.5 kg/3 lb. 5 oz.)
1 teaspoon salt
1 tablespoon coarsely ground
black pepper
½ tablespoon sugar
3 garlic cloves, chopped
½ tablespoon ground cinnamon
3 sticks of cinnamon (7.5 cm/
3 inches long)
3 dried bay leaves
½ tablespoon whole black
peppercorns
a small pinch of freshly grated
nutmeg
6 whole cloves
2 tablespoons tomato purée/paste
2 ripe on-the-vine tomatoes,
chopped
250 ml/1 cup red wine
⅓ cup red wine vinegar
olive oil, for cooking
mashed potatoes, to serve
a small handful of freshly chopped
flat-leaf parsley, to garnish

SERVES 4

Preheat the oven to 160°C (325°F) Gas 3.

First prepare the baby onions. The easiest method (and to avoid crying in the kitchen) is to trim the stalk-end of them, cut a small X into the end, put them all in a bowl and pour over boiling water. Cover and leave for 10 minutes, after which time drain, refresh with cold water and then you'll find that you can easily peel off the onion skins, leaving the onions whole.

To prepare the stifado, season the beef ribs with the salt, pepper and sugar. Fry the ribs in a lidded ovenproof pan (or casserole) in a little oil just to brown them on all sides, about 10 minutes, then remove from the pan. Pour away any excess fat from the pan and add a few glugs of olive oil.

Add the peeled onions and fry until they start to brown, then add the garlic. After a couple of minutes, add the ground cinnamon, cinnamon sticks, bay leaves, peppercorns, nutmeg, cloves, tomato purée and chopped fresh tomatoes. Cook this out for a few minutes before adding the wine and vinegar.

Turn the heat up and reduce the wine by half. Return the ribs to the pan and pour in enough water to almost cover them, but not quite. Bring to the boil and then cover tightly and place in the preheated oven for at least 3 hours, perhaps 4 hours, depending on the size and thickness of your ribs.

When the ribs are fork-tender, remove the pan from the oven and let it rest for 15 minutes. If the stew is too loose, remove the ribs from the pan, spoon off any excess fat from the surface and bring to a simmer on the hob/stovetop to reduce the sauce just enough to help it thicken. Reintroduce the ribs to the pan and baste with the sauce.

Serve the ribs on top of creamy mashed potatoes and spoon over some of the sauce, ensuring everyone gets plenty of baby onions. Garnish with the freshly chopped parsley.

SLOW-COOKED MEATS
kleftiko

The name *kleftiko* is derived from the Greek word *klepto*, which means to steal (which is where the English word kleptomaniac comes from). *Kleftiko* is the infamous 'stolen meat'. Legend has it that the bandits in Cyprus would steal a goat and take it up to the Troodos Mountains, where their hideaways were. To avoid being caught, they would dig a large pit and make a fire during the day when the flames wouldn't be seen. Once the fire had died leaving just the glowing embers, the beast would be placed on top of the ashes, covered and left until the next day. The ultimate and original slow-cooking...

The oven method here not only gives great results but also keeps you on the right side of the law! I've given a recipe for goat shoulder here for authenticity but it also works spectacularly well with lamb shoulder. Serve both these kleftikos with chunks of good bread to mop up the delicious juices, a crisp green salad and a bowl of tangy Greek olives.

LAMB SHOULDER KLEFTIKO
arni kleftiko

Lamb can be easier to source than goat and does tend to yield more meat. A shoulder of lamb is a tough cut, but it rewards you the most when you slow cook it. Personally, I never use any other cut for *kleftiko* as it ensures fall-off-the bone succulence.

2 onions, thickly sliced
1 garlic bulb, broken into cloves
6 sprigs of fresh rosemary
6 sprigs of fresh thyme
2 large ripe tomatoes, thickly sliced
1 tablespoon Greek dried oregano
2 kg/4½ lb. lamb shoulder (whole)
6 Cyprus potatoes, cut into quarters lengthways
freshly squeezed juice of ½ lemon
1 tablespoon smoked paprika
100 ml/⅓ cup white wine
salt and freshly ground black pepper
olive oil, for drizzling

SERVES 6–8

Preheat the oven to 160°C (325°F) Gas 3.

Prepare the lamb and other ingredients following the method for Kid Goat Kleftiko (see right).

Cook in the preheated oven for 4 hours. Once done, remove from the oven and rest for 15 minutes while still sealed. While resting, turn the oven up to 230°C (450°F) Gas 8.

Once the oven is to temperature, remove the foil and baking parchment, baste the lamb with some of the juices and put back in the oven for 5 minutes to help colour the meat.

To serve, decant the lamb onto a platter along with the potatoes. Pour the cooking juices into a bowl, skim off the fat, then drizzle the juices over the lamb.

KID GOAT KLEFTIKO
katsiki kleftiko

Goat meat has been part of our culture and cuisine since the Ancient Greeks and still deserves a place on our kitchen tables now, more than ever. Goat meat is incredibly healthy and lean (lower in fat and cholesterol than beef, lamb, pork and even chicken) and high in iron and protein. Still very popular in many continents, kid goat is very sustainable and puts to good use an animal that otherwise goes to waste. But I also love it because it tastes fabulous. Kid goat is packed with flavour and very versatile, it is lean so works well when slow cooked and this is the perfect recipe to get you started.

2 onions, thickly sliced
1 garlic bulb, broken into cloves
6 sprigs of fresh rosemary
6 sprigs of fresh thyme
2 large ripe tomatoes, thickly sliced
1 tablespoon Greek dried oregano
2-kg/4¹/₂-lb. kid goat shoulder (whole)
6 Cyprus potatoes, cut into quarters lengthways
freshly squeezed juice of ¹/₂ lemon
1 tablespoon smoked paprika
100 ml/¹/₃ cup white wine
salt and freshly ground black pepper
olive oil, for drizzling

SERVES 6–8

Preheat the oven to 160°C (325°F) Gas 3.

Drizzle a little olive oil into a roasting pan and scatter in the onions, garlic, half the rosemary, half the thyme and half the sliced tomatoes. Add a pinch of salt and pepper and half the oregano.

Place the goat shoulder onto the onions. Arrange the potatoes around the edges.

Drizzle a little olive oil over the whole pan along with the lemon juice. Season the meat and potatoes with the smoked paprika, the remaining oregano, thyme and rosemary, and a generous pinch of salt and pepper. Place the remaining tomato slices over the meat.

Add the wine and 50 ml/3¹/₂ tablespoons water into the pan (not over the goat) and cover with a piece of parchment paper, tucking the edges inside the roasting pan and then covering the whole pan with foil, ensuring it is tightly sealed around the edges (you may need to use a couple of sheets).

Cook in the preheated oven for 3 hours. Once done, remove from the oven and rest for 15 minutes while still sealed. While resting, turn the oven up to 230°C (450°F) Gas 8.

Once the oven is to temperature, remove the foil and baking parchment, baste the goat with some of the juices and put back in the oven for 5 minutes to help colour the meat.

To serve, decant the goat onto a platter along with the potatoes. Pour the cooking juices into a bowl and skim off the fat, then drizzle the juices over the goat.

RED WINE MARINATED PORK WITH CORIANDER SEEDS
afelia

Afelia is a Cypriot speciality of pork loin marinated in red wine and coriander seeds, creating a unique flavour. I have memories of eating this at my Yiayia's London home as a child. It was part of the ritual of my visits to turn up at her house, get a kiss (that I would immediately wipe off with the cute indignation that only a six-year-old can pull off) and scamper through the legs of giants straight to the fridge, pull the door open with both hands and then just stand and stare; gazing into the cold wondering what treasures lay within. *Afelia* was one such treasure. My Yiayia pan-fried pork loin, my version is slow-cooked using the shoulder. It takes longer, but the prize is tender meat in a rich stew.

1 kg/2¼ lb. skinned pork shoulder, cut into large chunks
500 ml/2 cups good red wine
2 dried bay leaves
1 tablespoon whole coriander seeds
1 tablespoon Greek honey
salt and freshly ground black pepper
olive oil, for frying
a handful of freshly chopped flat-leaf parsley, to garnish
1 tablespoon coriander seeds, toasted and coarsely crushed, to garnish
sea salt flakes, to serve
boiled rice or crusty bread, to serve

SERVES 6

Preheat the oven to 180°C (360°F) Gas 4.

Cut the pork shoulder into chunks the size of golf balls. Place in a bowl with the red wine, bay leaves and the whole coriander seeds. Place in the fridge to marinate for anything from 30 minutes to overnight.

When you're ready to cook the pork, remove the pork from the marinade (reserving the marinade) and pat it dry. There will be coriander seeds stuck to the pork and that's fine. Season the meat well. Heat a little oil in a lidded ovenproof pan and pan-fry the pork in batches over a high heat to brown the meat.

Put all the meat back into the pan, pour in the marinade, add the honey and bring to a simmer. Cover and cook in the preheated oven for about 1½ hours.

When you remove the pan from the oven, the sauce will look a little dull in colour. The magic happens when you place the pan back on the hob/stovetop and bring it to a simmer on a high heat for a few minutes. The sauce will reduce a little, thicken and become much glossier.

Serve garnished with the chopped parsley, the toasted and crushed coriander seeds and a pinch of sea salt flakes. I usually eat this with some plain boiled rice or crusty bread to offset the richness of the dish.

CREAMY CHICKEN RISOTTO
WITH CRISPY CRACKLING
avgolemoni rizoto me krotides kotopoulou

Avgolemoni soup is food for the soul made by Greek mothers the world over. It is a warming broth that legend has it can fix anything from a broken leg to a broken heart. I'm not sure on the medical evidence of the leg-fixing abilities, but it is definitely an emotional crutch served in bowls. My risotto dish is loosely based on this humble soup, but made heartier using the creamy starch of Arborio rice to thicken and enrich instead of the traditional eggs.

2 boneless chicken breasts, skin on
$^1/_2$ chicken stock/bouillon cube
1 small onion or 2 shallots,
   finely diced
$^1/_2$ celery stick/stalk, finely diced
2 garlic cloves, sliced
1 bay leaf
a generous pinch Greek dried
   oregano, crumbled
300 g/generous 1$^1/_2$ cups Arborio
   rice
125 ml/$^1/_2$ cup white wine
200 g/7 oz. halloumi cheese
15 g/1 tablespoon butter
finely grated zest and freshly
   squeezed juice of 1 lemon
salt and freshly ground black
   pepper
olive oil, for cooking and drizzling
a few fresh oregano leaves,
   to garnish

SERVES 4

Preheat the oven to 220°C (425°F) Gas 7.

First make the chicken-skin shards. Peel off the skin from the chicken breasts and place it between two sheets of baking parchment, ensuring the skin is stretched out. Season with a little salt. Place onto a baking sheet and place another baking sheet on top. Bake in the preheated oven for 15 minutes. Once cooked, remove the skins from the parchment, season again with salt, and set aside to cool, ideally on a wire rack or paper towels.

Poach the chicken breasts in 1.5 litres/quarts of water with the stock cube for about 10 minutes or until cooked through, skimming off any impurities every so often. Leave the chicken breasts to rest in the stock until you are ready to cook the risotto. When you are ready, remove the breasts from the stock, cover them and chill until needed. Reheat the stock.

Fry the onion and celery in olive oil for 5–6 minutes until softened. Add the garlic, bay leaf and dried oregano. After 1 minute, add the rice, stir, then pour in the wine and gently simmer until reduced by half. Once reduced, start adding the warm stock one ladleful at a time, stirring the rice until it is almost cooked but with some bite left; this will take 25–30 minutes. You will not need all the stock for cooking but keep any left over.

Chop the cooked chicken, dice half the halloumi and add both to the rice. Continue cooking and stirring until the rice is done. It will thicken after cooking, so ensure it is very loose. Turn off the heat and let it rest. Fold in the butter, season well and add lemon juice to taste. Serve in bowls (loosened with a little hot stock if necessary). Grate the remaining halloumi over the top, scatter over the lemon zest and fresh oregano and drizzle with olive oil. Stab a few shards of the chicken skin into each bowl.

PORK FILLET WITH SMOKY WHITE BEANS & PICKLED APRICOT SALSA

hirino fileto me verikoko salsa kai fasolia

Rustic yet delicate and beautiful, this dish is inspired by *fasolia*, a white bean soup. The pork fillet is brined first to keep it moist, and then dusted with cinnamon and paprika which complements the tangy pickled apricot salsa.

BRINE
2 heaped tablespoons salt
1 tablespoon sugar

PORK FILLET
500-g/1-lb. 2 oz. pork fillet
a pinch of ground cinnamon
a pinch of paprika
freshly ground black pepper
olive oil, for frying

FASOLIA
100 g/3½ oz. smoked pork lardons
1 onion, finely diced
1 stick/stalk celery, finely diced
2 garlic cloves, finely sliced
2 dried bay leaves
290 g/2 cups drained canned
    cannellini beans
a splash of white wine
500 ml/2 cups chicken stock
a small handful of freshly chopped
    flat-leaf parsley
freshly squeezed juice of ½ lemon
salt and freshly ground black
    pepper

PICKLED APRICOT SALSA
4 soft dried apricots
1 tablespoon finely diced red onion
a pinch of freshly chopped flat-leaf
    parsley
1 tablespoon olive oil
a glug of sherry vinegar

SERVES 4

For the brine, combine the salt and sugar in a large bowl and add 500 ml/2 cups of cold water and stir until fully dissolved. Add the pork fillet to the bowl and leave to brine for 1 hour before cooking. When you are ready to cook the meat, remove it from the brine, rinse and pat dry.

Preheat the oven to 200°C (400°F) Gas 6.

Dust the brined meat with the cinnamon, paprika and black pepper. Heat a little olive oil in a pan and sear the meat on all sides until browned. Transfer the meat to a roasting pan and cook in the preheated oven for 15 minutes, then remove and let it rest for 10 minutes before carving into thick equal portions.

Meanwhile, for the fasolia, fry the pork lardons in a little olive oil until crispy, then remove from the pan and reserve. Pour away any excess fat and replace with a drizzle of fresh olive oil. Fry the onion and celery for a few minutes until the onion has softened. Add the garlic and bay leaves, and let them mingle with the onions and celery for just a minute before adding the beans and wine. Simmer until the wine is reduced by half, then top with the stock. Cover with a lid and simmer for about 10 minutes or until the beans have softened. Once the beans are soft, remove the lid and let the sauce reduce until it resembles a thick casserole in consistency. If it gets too dry, add a splash of water.

Add the cooked lardons to the beans with the chopped parsley, season generously with salt and pepper and keep warm until ready to serve.

For the pickled apricot salsa, chop the dried apricots into small cubes and put into a bowl. Add the finely chopped red onion and parsley. Add the olive oil, a decent glug of vinegar, and season with salt and pepper. Leave to marinate for a few minutes before serving.

To serve, spoon the fasolia into serving bowls, place a pork fillet portion on top and finish with a few teaspoons of the pickled apricot salsa.

HALFWAY 'PASTITSIO'
miso-pastitsio

When my brothers and I were kids, my mum would make *pastitsio* – a Cypriot speciality, delicious served warm from the oven, or as a cold *meze*, cut into cubes. Her recipe called for a simple mix of cooked pasta tubes, minced pork and parsley, sometimes with a hint of ground cinnamon, all topped with a white sauce before being baked in the oven. There was always some left over pasta and mince at the halfway stage that we would scoff down in a shot, so this recipe pays homage to that. While I was working on developing the recipes for this book, my children, Eva, Lex and Luca made the best tasters, and this particular idea passed with flying colours. And I completely understand why...

2 large onions, finely diced
350 g/12 oz. minced/ground pork
1 cinnamon stick, about 7.5 cm/
    3 inches long
1 teaspoon ground cinnamon
a handful of freshly chopped
    flat-leaf parsley
400 g/14 oz. dried spaghetti pasta
1 stock/bouillon cube (meat or
    vegetable)
salt and freshly ground black
    pepper
olive oil, for cooking and drizzling
sea salt flakes, to garnish

SERVES 4

Pour enough olive oil into a frying pan/skillet to just cover the base and then gently fry the onions on a low heat. You need to take some time with the onions, you want to cook them slowly so they release their sugars and gently caramelize without burning, so this will take about 10 minutes. Once the onions are done, remove them from the pan and reserve.

In the same pan, add the minced pork and cinnamon stick and fry on a high heat until the mince is cooked through and just starting to caramelize. Once the pork is cooked through and some of it starts to look crispy, turn the heat down a little and reintroduce the onions to the pan, followed by the ground cinnamon, a generous amount of salt and pepper and the chopped parsley. Fold it all together and if the pasta isn't ready yet, turn off the heat.

Cook the pasta in boiling water according to the packet instructions, but with the addition of the stock cube. Once the pasta is cooked, drain it, reserving a little of the cooking water. Add the pasta to the minced pork pan with a few tablespoons of the cooking liquid and be sure to scrape the bottom of the pan to release all the sticky dark bits into the sauce.

Simmer the pasta in with the pork until the liquid has almost all evaporated, leaving just a silky coating to the pasta – this is a dry dish, so don't expect a ragú.

Serve dressed with a drizzle of olive oil and a pinch of sea salt flakes.

'BIRD'S NEST' POUSSIN
kotopoulo folias

This is a dish for when you want to impress. Delicate little poussins, stuffed with aromatic herbs, dusted with sumac and sitting on nests of *kadayif* pastry. The nests add a crunch which contrasts with the moist flesh of the birds, and a light sauce brings it all together. Serve with a green salad and smug expression.

200 g/7 oz. kadayif pastry
1 tablespoon Greek dried oregano
a handful of fresh sage leaves
a bunch of fresh basil leaves
  (Greek basil if available)
a bunch of fresh oregano leaves
4 poussins (about 450 g/1 lb. each)
1 lemon
4 garlic cloves, unpeeled but
  cracked
a small bunch of fresh thyme
4 dried bay leaves
2 tablespoons sumac
a pinch of sugar
1 tablespoon cornflour/cornstarch,
  mixed with a little cold water to
  make a slurry just before using
2 tablespoons dried edible flowers,
  crumbled (see Tip on page 165)
salt and freshly ground black
  pepper
olive oil, for oiling and drizzling

4 simple bowl-shape foil moulds,
  slightly bigger than the poussin

SERVES 4

Preheat the oven to 180°C (360°F) Gas 4.

First make the nests. Place your foil bowls in a high-sided roasting pan. Lay out the kadayif pastry in thin strips about 2.5 cm/1 inch wide. Season with salt and pepper and scatter over the dried oregano. Arrange one strip in a ring at the bottom of one of the foil bowls. Lightly oil the sage leaves (I just use oiled fingertips). Lay a couple of leaves over the pastry. Repeat with a second slightly wider ring of pastry, resting it on top of the first. Add a few more oiled sage leaves. Repeat to create four nests, using one-quarter of the pastry and sage for each one and aiming for as much height as possible. (Manipulate the foil a little to get the shape you want.)

Transfer the nests in the roasting pan to the preheated oven and bake them for 10–12 minutes, until they start to colour and crisp up. Remove from the oven, carefully as they are fragile. Gently insert small basil and oregano leaves into each nest and set aside until ready to serve.

Season the inside of each poussin and place in a roasting pan. Quarter the lemon, squeeze the juice over each bird then place the used lemon quarters inside each one, followed by a garlic clove, a few sprigs of thyme and a bay leaf. Drizzle with a little olive oil, season again and dust with the sumac. Roast in the still-hot oven for 20–25 minutes, then let them rest for 10 minutes. After resting, place the birds on a chopping board and pour the cooking juices back into the roasting pan. Either leave the birds whole (as shown) or quarter them as preferred; first lengthways along the breast bone and then between the breast and the leg. Cover with foil.

To make a gravy-style sauce, deglaze the roasting pan with a little water or white wine if you have any. Add the sugar and the cornflour slurry. Heat, stirring until it thickens, and then pass through a sieve/strainer.

To assemble, carefully place each nest on a serving plate and sprinkle the dried-flower crumb around the edge, add the poussin (either whole or piled in pieces) and spoon a little of the warm sauce over the birds only.

TEN CLOVES GARLIC LEMON CHICKEN
kotopoulo lemonato me skordo

This may seem like a lot of garlic, but trust me, it slowly melts away and just becomes another thread woven into the tapestry of flavours in the dish. The taste of it evokes warm memories of evening suppers I've enjoyed in many Greek kitchens, nothing fancy, just good, honest ingredients playing nicely together. This is a great recipe for feeding a hungry family.

12 chicken thighs, skin on, bone in
10 garlic cloves, thickly sliced
3 courgettes/zucchini, quartered
   lengthways and then cut into
   2.5-cm/1-inch slices
a generous splash of white wine
3 dried bay leaves
a handful of green and purple
   Kalamata olives, pitted
   (see Tip, right)
a generous couple of pinches of
   Greek dried oregano
1/2 stock/bouillon cube (chicken
   or vegetable)
a generous pinch of sugar
2 lemons
a handful of freshly chopped
   flat-leaf parsley (optional)
salt and freshly ground black
   pepper
olive oil, for cooking and drizzling
Bulgur Wheat & Vermicelli
   Noodles (see page 113)
   or boiled rice, to serve

SERVES 6

Season the chicken thighs with salt and pepper, then fry them skin-side down in a little olive oil over a high heat in a large, ovenproof frying pan/ skillet, turning once to ensure they are golden all over. (You may need to cook them in batches.)

Remove from the pan, reduce the heat to very low and pour away most of the chicken fat leaving a tablespoon or two. Add all the garlic and cook on a low heat, stirring occasionally, ensuring it doesn't burn. After about 5–6 minutes, add the courgette, cook for a few minutes and then pour in the wine. Simmer until the liquid has reduced by half then add the sugar, bay leaves, olives and oregano. Add 250 ml/1 cup of water with the stock cube and stir it in to dissolve.

Return the seared chicken thighs to the pan, skin-side up, trying not to get the skin wet. Squeeze the juice of 1 lemon all over the chicken. Cut the other lemon into quarters and arrange the wedges sporadically in the pan. Drizzle a little more olive oil on top of the chicken, season again and place the whole pan in the preheated oven for about 35–40 minutes.

Remove the pan from the oven, scatter fresh parsley over the top, if using, and serve. Personally, I like to bring the whole pan to the table. This is good served with Bulgur Wheat & Vermicelli Noodles (Pougouri) or just a bowl of boiled rice.

Tip: Pitted olives tend to be dry and flavourless. It really pays to buy whole olives and, with the flat side of a blade, push down to remove the pits. But don't get hung up on it, life's too short. If you only have pitted to hand, use those.

sun

SUN
ilios

Another childhood trip to Cyprus – this time the occasion is a wedding, a Greek wedding is one thing, a Greek wedding in a village in Cyprus is something else entirely, but this isn't about a wedding. This is about an old man, a pair of boots and a curious kid. I am outside my great-aunt's house. It's hot and wafts of mirrored air rise from the dusty earth under my feet. I am walking behind an old Greek man. I can't recall now how I ended up tottering along behind him. I imagine it was (as usual) born out of boredom, intrigue and mischief. This particular morning I had already spent an hour riding a moped around the village with only a T-shirt and the confidence of youth for protection; pinched a few mouthfuls of food from the kitchen (not out of hunger, just for the thrill of being chased by a screaming great aunt) and tried unsuccessfully to capture several lizards. I was fast running out of entertainment options. It was 9 am... I had spotted the man a few minutes earlier. He was wearing standard issue elderly-Greek-man attire; vest and shirt tucked into belted trousers, but this time accessorized with a pair of knee-high leather boots, a few shades darker

but no less creased with age than his sun-weathered face. His shovel-sized hands carried a long wooden stick and just visible was a catapult hanging out of his back trouser pocket. I am in – this has adventure written all over it... I drop everything and run after him. I know he knows I'm there as I'm walking right behind him, yet he ignores me. But I'm not bothered by this, I'm far more interested in finding out what mission we are on. It seems we are heading past the house and towards a large vegetable patch. Weaving through the plants he suddenly, and violently, whacks the ground with his stick. I jump back in surprise, starting to feel concerned that I might be following in the footsteps of a madman! There's nothing there that I can see except earth and vegetables, yet the stick whacking continues periodically. My initial concern then evaporates in the heat of the morning sun into pure entertainment. Skipping along, I giggle and snigger with each thwack, which is in turn followed by the swivel of his head and a disapproving glance. Eventually I decide to enlighten this poor soul with the wisdom of a 10-year-old city kid standing in a field. My

chest puffed out, hands on my hips and with an air of authority I impart the knowledge that there is nothing there to be hit! He stops walking and slowly turns round. He then speaks for the first time, replying with three terrifying words that render me speechless.

'Scares away snakes'. This is the precise moment that my silent gaping-hole face was invented. Now we are on speaking terms, he is quick, no delighted, to inform me that the boots he is sporting stop the snakes from biting him and gives them an affectionate little tap with the end of his stick for emphasis. Checkmate. He waits for my response, cocky little kid. My head drops and my gaze travels beyond my shorts to my feet, little sun-tanned toes barely concealed inside my jelly shoes and feel alarmingly underdressed. I look up and without a word make an about-turn and walk, then jog, then run back to the safety of the house. I never did find out what the catapult was for, which with hindsight was probably a good thing. Cultivating patches of land was, and in some areas still is, part of daily Cypriot and Greek life. It's serious stuff, rather than a weekend allotment that produces a glut

of beans that you share with your neighbours, this is what provides food for the family. A combination of sun, earth, dedication and hard work allied to enable families to grow what forms the mainstay of their diets and provide vital sustenance. *Horta* (wild greens) wilted and served with a golden drizzle of local extra-virgin olive oil and a squeeze of sun-kissed lemon juice; sweet figs eaten straight off the tree; gnarled cucumbers destined to be diced and paired with tomatoes, so sun-ripened their aroma acts as an olfactory map to lead you to their hiding place. Glossy red onions and plump Cyprus potatoes pulled from the red earth to be roasted with Greek oregano (considered to be the best in the world). Silky leeks, green beans, mint and parsley plus olives, honey, *mastiha* and natural wines made from locally-grown grapes, these are humble foods, the true fruits of the earth.

Unquestionably, things have changed over the generations: affluence, a reduction in private land and all-year-round availability of imported ingredients – but the celebration of this simple and honest produce still provides the foundations of Greek cuisine today.

FLOWER & HERB SALAD
salada agrion botanigon kai loulouthia

This fresh and fragrant salad is basically summertime in a bowl. The herbs and baby salad leaves create a wonderful green garden backdrop to the bursts of colour and scent coming from the flowers.

3 spring onions/scallions
150 g/5$^1/_2$ oz. baby salad leaves (such as spinach, kale and chard, nothing too peppery)
a handful of freshly chopped flat-leaf parsley
a handful of freshly chopped coriander/cilantro
$^1/_2$ handful of fresh basil, ripped
a handful of freshly chopped mint
$^1/_2$ handful of freshly chopped dill
4 tablespoons olive oil
3 tablespoons balsamic vinegar
a few drops of freshly squeezed lemon juice
a generous pinch of Greek dried oregano
a punnet of edible flowers (see Tip on page 165)
salt and freshly ground black pepper

SERVES 6

Trim the ends off the spring onions, finely slice the entire length and place in a large mixing bowl with the salad leaves and fresh herbs. Pour over the olive oil, vinegar and a little squeeze of lemon juice.

Season with salt and pepper and the dried oregano, and then just before serving, toss in the flowers (saving a few of the prettiest ones to garnish).

Decant into a serving bowl, shaking off any excess dressing, and scatter the remaining flowers over the top to garnish.

FETA & MINT GREENS
horta me feta kai thiosmi

There is something about the simplicity of this recipe that just works. Sweet petits pois, salty feta, earthy spinach. It couldn't be easier to make and goes with just about everything.

500 g/4 cups petits pois
125 g/2$^1/_2$ cups baby spinach leaves
5 g/$^1/_4$ cup freshly chopped mint
5 g/$^1/_4$ cup freshly chopped flat-leaf parsley
a pinch of dried chilli/hot red pepper flakes
a few drops of freshly squeezed lemon juice
150 g/5$^1/_2$ oz. feta cheese, roughly crumbled
salt and freshly ground black pepper
olive oil, for drizzling

SERVES 6

Simmer the petits pois in a pan of lightly salted water until just cooked through. Drain and immediately fold through the spinach, allowing the residual heat in the petits pois to wilt the spinach.

Once the steam has evaporated, stir through the herbs and chilli flakes, add the lemon juice and season with some salt and pepper.

Drizzle over some olive oil and stir in the feta. Keep the pieces of feta quite chunky, as they will break down even further when mixed.

Serve whilst warm.

WATERMELON & HALLOUMI BOWLS
karpouzi kai haloumi kypella

I remember on one visit to my parents' village in Cyprus we started the day with simple plates of sweet watermelon, salty halloumi and a little fresh *koulouri*, a ridge-backed loaf of bread covered in sesame and fennel seeds. It was a casual, communal affair, with everyone grazing on the shared food. There's an art to enjoying the simple pleasures in life, and to me this is one of them. Inspired by that memorable breakfast, here is a simple salad that is good for any time of the day, and can also be enjoyed at the end of a meal.

500 g/1 lb. 2 oz. halloumi cheese
a handful of fresh mint
½ red onion
3 small watermelons
a pinch of chilli/chili powder

SERVES 6

Cut the halloumi into bite-sized chunks. Rip all the mint leaves from the stalks and finely slice the red onion.

Cut one-third off each watermelon (lengthways if it's not perfectly round) and scoop out the flesh from each side. Cut any large pieces into more manageable sizes. Dust the melon flesh with a little chilli powder, scatter most of the mint leaves over the melon and place it in a bowl.

With the smaller piece of each watermelon, you should have what looks like a shallow red and green salad bowl in front of you (you can thinly slice a little from the bottom to help it stand without wobbling about). Then simply fill it with layers of watermelon, halloumi and red onion, and scatter the remaining mint leaves on top.

Just to clarify, these don't need to be separate layers, you just want to avoid mixing this like a normal salad, as the watermelon will start to break down. Just place it in gently and serve immediately.

GREEK NEW POTATO SALAD
ellenikes patates neos

These are garlicky and zesty and the freshness of the mint brings them alive. It is a wonderful accompaniment to any big feast. Oh, and the leftovers taste fabulous fried in the morning with a couple of eggs and some chillies thrown into the pan.

1 kg/2¼ lb. waxy new potatoes, such as Charlottes
a small knob/pat of butter
60 ml/¼ cup olive oil, for dressing
1 tablespoon cider vinegar
freshly squeezed juice of ¼ lemon
2 garlic cloves, crushed to a paste
a pinch of Greek dried oregano
a handful of fresh mint leaves
½ red onion, finely sliced
salt and freshly ground black pepper

SERVES 6

Bring a large pan of salted water to the boil and cook the new potatoes for about 10 minutes, or until you can pierce with a knife with little resistance. Drain the potatoes and throw in the butter while they steam dry.

Mix together the olive oil, vinegar, lemon juice, garlic and oregano, and generously add some salt and pepper. Pour this dressing over the potatoes, ensuring they are well coated, then finely slice half the mint and add to the potatoes with the onion.

When you're ready to serve, move the potatoes to a clean serving dish, leaving any excess liquid behind. Taste to ensure the seasoning and tartness is right (we call this 'chef's privileges'!) and scatter the remaining whole mint leaves over the top.

CYPRUS LEMON POTATOES
kypriakes patates me lemoni

Cyprus potatoes are delicious. You can spot them immediately as they proudly wear their little suits of red soil from the rich earth they grew in. They are waxy with a slight chewiness to them and when roasted they take on a wonderfully creamy flavour.

1 kg/2¼ lb. Cyprus potatoes
4 garlic cloves, thickly sliced
125 ml/½ cup olive oil, for roasting
125 ml/½ cup white wine
1 lemon
2 generous pinches of Greek dried oregano
salt and freshly ground black pepper

23 x 30-cm/9 x 12-inch roasting pan

SERVES 6

Preheat the oven to 180°C (360°F) Gas 4.

Peel the potatoes and then cut into quarters lengthways. Place them in the roasting pan, followed by the garlic. Now pour in the olive oil, wine and 125 ml/½ cup of water. Halve the lemon and squeeze in the juice, then throw the leftover lemon into the pan as well. Finally, add a couple of pinches of oregano and season generously with salt and pepper.

Place the potatoes into the oven for about an hour, or just over, depending how crispy you want them. Turn the potatoes once halfway through cooking to help brown the different sides.

You want to make sure when you add the potatoes to the roasting pan that the liquid is only about halfway up the potatoes; they are meant to be roasted, not boiled. Once cooked, give them another sprinkle of salt and serve.

GREEK SALAD
ellenike salada

If there's one dish that epitomizes Greek cuisine, it's the Greek salad. Incredibly fresh ingredients, minimal preparation and mother nature taking all the credit. When it comes to creating something as simple and elegant as a Greek salad, you must buy the best quality ingredients you can afford and spend time choosing your produce. Tomatoes are, without a doubt, the headline act of this show, so look for on-the-vine fruits that are vibrant red, look like they are about to burst their skins and, importantly, have a smell. If you can't smell them, you won't taste them either. Greek Kalamata olives should be bought whole – an olive's stone is its soul, and once it loses that it just won't taste the same. And of course, the oil, make sure it's a fruity one from Greece or Cyprus, extra-virgin and the best you can lay your hands on.

6 ripe and fragrant on-the-vine
    tomatoes
1/2 red onion
1 cucumber
1/2 green (bell) pepper
50 g/1/2 cup Kalamata olives
a pinch of fresh coriander/cilantro
    leaves
a generous pinch of Greek dried
    oregano, plus extra to serve
200 g/7 oz. feta cheese
salt and freshly ground black
    pepper
olive oil, for drizzling
red wine vinegar, for drizzling

**SERVES 2 AS A MAIN,
6 AS A SIDE DISH**

Cut the tomatoes into chunks about 2.5–5 cm/1–2 inches in size and place into a bowl. Thinly slice the red onion and break it up on top of the tomatoes. Quarter the cucumber lengthways, rest it on its side and run a teaspoon along the length to remove the seeds, but don't worry if you don't, this is meant to be rustic. Slice the cucumber into chunks about the same size as the tomatoes. If you are using small cucumbers that are bent and twisted and bear the markings of their vegetable-patch birthplace, just chop them, they taste the best.

Halve the green pepper, remove any pith and seeds, and finely slice it from top to bottom. Put it in with the rest. Throw in the olives and a pinch of fresh coriander leaves.

Generously shower the salad in olive oil, then about the same in red wine vinegar. Dust in the oregano and a little salt and pepper. Gently fold everything together (with your hands if you like) and then decant into a serving bowl, leaving behind some of the excess liquid.

Finally, break up the feta into big chunks over the top, and top with another drizzle of olive oil and vinegar, and an extra sprinkling of oregano.

GREEK VEGETABLE TART
salada lahaniki tarta

This simple yet handsome tart relys on classic sunshine flavours and colours to create a quick and delicious bite to eat. It works wonderfully as a light lunch with just a few dressed green leaves on the side, or can be popped on the table for all to share. I buy ready-made puff pastry and, if I'm totally honest, I usually grab the pre-rolled variety for utter convenience as well . Sometimes you just have to be a little Machiavellian about things!

350 g/12 oz. ready-made puff pastry
1 courgette/zucchini
1/2 aubergine/eggplant
1/2 red Romano pepper, deseeded
1/4 red onion
a generous pinch of Greek dried oregano
a generous pinch of ground cumin
12 baby plum tomatoes
50 g/1³/4 oz. halloumi cheese
2 tablespoons pine nut kernels
1 tablespoon Greek honey
125 g/¹/2 cup Greek yogurt
70 g/2¹/2 oz. feta cheese
salt and freshly ground black pepper
olive oil, for drizzling
a few sprigs of basil, to garnish (Greek basil if available)

25 x 38-cm/10 x 15-inch baking sheet, lined with baking parchment

SERVES 6–8

Preheat the oven to 200°C (400°F) Gas 6.

Roll out the puff pastry (if necessary) so that it fits snugly on the prepared baking sheet. Using a sharp knife, lightly score all the way round about 2.5 cm/1 inch inside the edge of the puff pastry and bake in the preheated oven for 10–12 minutes, or until the pastry has puffed up and started to turn golden. Once the puff pastry is cooked, remove from the oven and let it cool slightly, before gently pushing down the centre of the pastry, leaving you with a little 'collar' around the edge.

To prepare the filling, dice the courgette, aubergine and pepper into about 2.5-cm/1-inch cubes and thinly slice the red onion. Drizzle with a little olive oil, season generously with the oregano, cumin and salt and pepper, and roast in the oven on a separate baking sheet for 10 minutes.

Quarter the baby plum tomatoes, grate the halloumi cheese and add both to the roasted vegetables, along with the pine nuts and honey.

When you are ready to assemble, dot the puff pastry base with a few spoonfuls of Greek yogurt and then distribute the mixed vegetables over the top, including on top of the yogurt. Try to keep the vegetables in one layer; if they are overloaded it will go a little soggy. Finally, crumble the feta in chunks on top, drizzle with a little olive oil and bake in the oven for a further 10 minutes just to help all the ingredients snuggle up together.

Once cooked, let it cool slightly and then garnish with a scattering of basil leaves and a good turn of black pepper.

BULGAR WHEAT & VERMICELLI NOODLES
pourgouri

Pourgouri, or bulgar wheat, is a staple of Cypriot cuisine and is used throughout Greece and the Eastern Mediterranean. Traditionally, it is a simple dish cooked in stock with broken vermicelli noodles throughout. My addition of chipotle flakes gives a nice smoky kick, and fresh coriander brings it to life.

½ small onion
25 g/⅓ cup broken vermicelli noodles
170 g/1 cup bulgar (cracked wheat), rinsed and drained
½ tablespoon tomato purée/paste
½ chicken stock/bouillon cube
2 generous pinches of dried chipotle flakes
2 tablespoons diced red onion
a small handful of fresh coriander/cilantro
salt and freshly ground black pepper
olive oil, for cooking

SERVES 4

Finely dice the brown onion and then fry in a little olive oil in a deep lidded pan until soft. Add the broken vermicelli noodles and continue to fry until the noodles start to brown but don't burn.

Add the rinsed bulgar to the pan, followed by the tomato purée, chicken stock cube and 350 ml/1½ cups of cold water.

Bring it to a simmer and as soon as it starts to bubble, cover with a lid, turn down the heat to the lowest setting and let it cook for 10 minutes. Turn off the heat and leave covered to sit for a further 10 minutes.

Fluff up the grains with a fork and, while still warm, add the chipotle flakes, diced red onion, some salt and pepper and an extra glug of olive oil.

If serving immediately, add the fresh coriander, otherwise, let it cool before adding the herbs to stop them wilting.

RIBBON SALAD
salada tis kordellas

There is something I find incredibly pleasing to the eye about this *carpaccio* inspired ribbon salad – elegant slithers of courgettes, carrots and asparagus, sensually tangled together on the plate, just waiting to be devoured...

1 green courgette/zucchini
1 yellow courgette/zucchini
2 long carrots
120 g/4^{1}/$_{4}$ oz. fresh asparagus
  spears
2 tablespoons rapeseed oil
2 tablespoons freshly squeezed
  lemon juice
a pinch of Greek dried oregano
^{1}/$_{2}$ teaspoon Dijon/French mustard
1 garlic clove
2 tablespoons toasted pine nut
  kernels
salt and freshly ground black
  pepper

SERVES 4

Top and tail the courgettes, peel and trim the carrots, and cut the tough ends off the asparagus spears.

Using a peeler, slice thin strips of the entire length of all the vegetables, ideally keeping a little bit of skin on either side of the courgette strips for colour, and place them into a mixing bowl.

Put the rapeseed oil, lemon juice, oregano and mustard into a jar, tighten the lid and shake until it emulsifies together into a dressing. Pour just enough of the dressing over the vegetable ribbons to coat, mixing gently to avoid breaking the ribbons.

Find a suitable serving dish, something big and flat. Peel the garlic clove, cut it in half and wipe the cut side over the inside of the serving dish. Discard the garlic. Gently decant the vegetables into the serving dish, shaking off any excess dressing.

Finally, scatter the toasted pine nuts over the top, season with salt and coarsely ground black pepper, and serve immediately.

ORZO, ROASTED TOMATO & FETA SALAD
salada kritharaki me frigmenes tomades kai feta

I've had an ongoing love affair with orzo for quite some time. Incredibly versatile, it's a tiny pasta shaped like rice that can be used in so many ways. In this salad, it's the juices from the roasted tomatoes that seep into the orzo and create a sumptuously smart dressing that works for me. Accessorized with pockets of melting feta, it not only looks the part, it also tastes great.

300 g/2 cups orzo pasta
a handful of baby plum tomatoes
a handful of fresh basil, torn
200 g/7 oz. feta cheese, crumbled
2 tablespoons pine nut kernels, toasted
finely grated zest and freshly squeezed juice of 1/2 lemon
salt and freshly ground black pepper
olive oil, for drizzling

SERVES 2 AS A MAIN, 6 AS A SIDE DISH

Preheat the oven to 180°C (360°F) Gas 4.

Simmer the orzo in plenty of boiling salted water for about 8 minutes or until just done – don't overcook it. Drain, rinse under cold running water and tip into a large bowl. Drizzle over a little olive oil to stop the 'grains' sticking together and set aside.

While the orzo is cooking, halve the tomatoes, place in an ovenproof dish, drizzle with olive oil and season with salt and pepper. Roast in the preheated oven for about 10 minutes or until they just start to char.

Pour the roasted tomatoes, including any juices, into the bowl with the cooked orzo, then add the torn basil, crumbled feta and a generous hit of ground black pepper.

Finish dressing the orzo with another drizzle of olive oil, then add the toasted pine nuts and lemon zest and juice – taste while you are adding this as you need only a touch of lemon juice.

OVEN-BAKED VEGETABLES WITH HARISSA
briam me harissa

As a child I never actually knew this dish had a name, I just enjoyed eating delicious slices of vegetables cooked in canned tomatoes. That's how it was done – nothing fancy, just local fresh ingredients, simply cooked. I'm not sure marrow is actually traditional in briam, but it's what we had so that's how I do it! Marrow flesh is quite unique with slithery strings of flesh enveloping the sauce, it plays well with the other vegetables. I find a little harissa stirred in works wonders, giving it subtle heat and making it more earthy in flavour.

2 aubergines/eggplants
3 potatoes
1 red onion
3 courgettes/zucchini
1 marrow/marrow squash
a generous pinch of Greek dried oregano
a small handful of freshly chopped flat-leaf parsley
2 tablespoons harissa paste
3 dried bay leaves
200-g/7-oz. can chopped tomatoes or equivalent weight of passata/ strained tomatoes
salt and freshly ground black pepper
olive oil, for drizzling

SERVES 6

Preheat the oven to 180°C (360°F) Gas 4.

Slice the aubergines, potatoes, onion, courgettes and marrow into 1.25-cm/$^1/_2$-inch discs, and drop into a mixing bowl. Drizzle in a few good glugs of olive oil and add the oregano, parsley, harissa paste and bay leaves. Fold everything through, ensuring all the ingredients have been touched by the oil and harissa. Season well and transfer to a roasting pan or ceramic ovenproof dish.

Scatter the chopped tomatoes or passata over the top. Cook uncovered in the preheated oven for about 1$^1/_2$ hours. Use a large spoon to gently turn over the vegetables after 1 hour to ensure even cooking and return to the oven.

Tip: I find this does vary slightly in cooking times, depending on the thickness of vegetables, the season, etc., but it's never taken less than 1 hour or more than 11/2 hours to cook. Feel free to remove it from the oven before 1$^1/_2$ hours is up if it everything is cooked.

STEWED FINE BEANS WITH NIGELLA SEEDS
fasolaki me nigella sporous

Fasolaki is a traditional dish that finds a home on every Greek table. Contrary to western methods of cooking green beans to keep them a little crisp, *fasolaki* is a slow cook and your patience is rewarded when the beans eventually submit to the heat of the tomato sauce and soften into a tangled aromatic stew. It's most often served as a side dish but can make a meal in itself, especially when diced potato is added, or as here, starchy broad beans. As a kid, I never enjoyed it but was made to eat it and now I take great pleasure in inflicting the same rule on my own children who (annoyingly) quite enjoy it! I like to splash Tabasco sauce over mine once it's served to add a bit of pep.

1 teaspoon nigella seeds
1/2 small onion, diced
1 garlic clove, chopped
500 g/1 lb. 2 oz. fine beans, stalks
    trimmed
120 g/1 cup shelled and peeled
    broad/fava beans
400-g/14-oz. can chopped
    tomatoes
a pinch of ground turmeric
a handful of freshly chopped
    flat-leaf parsley
salt and freshly ground black
    pepper
olive oil, for cooking and drizzling
crumbled feta, to serve (optional)

SERVES 6

Start by lightly toasting the nigella seeds in a dry frying pan/skillet for a minute to release their flavour. Remove them from the pan and set aside to garnish the dish at the end.

In the same pan, fry the onion in a little olive oil until golden, this takes about 5 minutes, then add the garlic. After another minute, add the fine beans and broad beans.

After a few minutes, when all the vegetables have introduced themselves to each other, add the chopped tomatoes, then fill the can one-third full with water and add that too. Add the turmeric and some salt and pepper.

Cover the pan and leave it to simmer gently for about 30 minutes. Check periodically and add more water if it needs it. After about 30 minutes, the fine beans should be nice and soft. At this point, remove the lid and let the sauce reduce until it is quite thick, if it isn't already.

Fold the chopped parsley into the stew, drizzle in a decent amount of olive oil and season again. Finish the dish by scattering over the nigella seeds. Crumble over some feta, if you like.

CYPRIOT SLOW-COOKED WHITE BEANS IN TOMATO SAUCE
fasolia

Fasolia goes by many different names, and versions of this honest peasant food are found all over the world. Each recipe originated because of what was grown in the area, but ultimately it is a white bean and tomato soup. The beans are soaked and then cooked slowly with vegetables to give flavour and body. I would be lying if I said that adding a handful of crispy pork lardons or slices of *pastourma* sausage doesn't add a little more depth to the dish, but I wanted to stay true to its humble roots.

1 small onion, finely diced
1 stick/¹/₂ cup thinly sliced celery, plus a few leaves, finely chopped, to garnish
80 g/¹/₂ cup freshly chopped tomatoes
1 tablespoon tomato purée/paste
135 g/1 cup grated carrot
a pinch of dried thyme
1 dried bay leaf
450 g/3 cups drained canned cannellini beans
a splash of white wine
750 ml/3 cups hot water
salt and freshly cracked black pepper
olive oil, for cooking and drizzling
a pinch of dried chilli/hot red pepper flakes, to garnish
a few drops of freshly squeezed lemon juice, to serve
bread, to serve

SERVES 4

Fry the onion and celery (not the leaves, save those for garnish) in a little olive oil on a low heat until the onion is soft and translucent, about 10 minutes.

Add the tomatoes and tomato purée, along with the carrot, thyme, bay and cannellini beans. Season generously with salt and plenty of cracked black pepper. Jiggle them all about a bit in the pan to get to know each other.

Add a splash of wine to the pan and reduce until almost gone, then top with the hot water. Bring to a simmer and cook for about 30 minutes, just to let the ingredients melt a little into each other.

This is best served the following day and reheated, but if you can't resist, let it rest for a while, then serve, garnished with finely chopped celery leaves, a pinch of dried chilli flakes, a little drizzle of olive oil, just a whisper of lemon juice and probably another hit of seasoning.

I serve this with nothing more than a chunk of bread and an appetite.

PORK & RICE-STUFFED VEGETABLES
gemista

There is nothing quite like a slow-cooked pepper filled with an aromatic stuffing of rice, meat, herbs and spices. When developing this recipe, I did what any self-respecting cookbook author should do – I phoned my mum. This was a staple dish when I was growing up and, a true amalgamation of our life in the UK and our Greek heritage, as it was always served with gravy. I love this recipe for its flexibility. You can stuff whatever you want: peppers, courgettes, beefsteak tomatoes, with whatever you like – minced pork, beef or lamb, or even leave it out for a vegetarian version. Have fun, cook it to your way and always, always, serve with gravy (and if you really must, a green salad as well).

6–8 vegetables for stuffing,
   I used 2 red (bell) peppers,
   2 courgettes/zucchini,
   2 beefsteak tomatoes,
   1 aubergine/eggplant
1 onion, diced
250 g/9 oz. minced/ground pork
2 generous pinches of ground
   cinnamon
1 tablespoon tomato purée/paste
150 g/generous 3/4 cup basmati
   rice
200 ml/scant 1 cup chicken stock
a small handful of toasted pine
   nut kernels
250 ml/1 cup canned chopped
   tomatoes or passata/strained
   tomatoes
a few handfuls of fresh herbs,
   always flat-leaf parsley, then
   whatever else you fancy,
   coriander/cilantro, mint, basil...
1 tablespoon Greek dried oregano
salt and freshly ground black
   pepper
olive oil, for cooking and drizzling
instant gravy, to serve (optional)

MAKES 6–8

Preheat the oven to 180°C (360°F) Gas 4.

Cut the top off each of the vegetables (save the tops for later) and scoop out the flesh inside. Place the vegetable bottoms into a roasting pan snug enough to hold them (I use a little crumpled foil underneath each vegetable to hold it upright).

To make the stuffing mixture, fry the diced onion in a pan with a little olive oil for 5 minutes until it softens and is cooked through. Add the minced pork and cook until done; if there is a lot of liquid, keep the heat on to reduce some of this.

Add the cinnamon, tomato purée and rice, and cook for a minute before adding the stock. Simmer gently until it is all absorbed – you're not cooking the rice, just giving it a little helping hand. Once the liquid has been absorbed, add the pine nuts, chopped tomatoes or passata and all the herbs. Season with salt and pepper and stir through. Turn off the heat.

Spoon this mixture into each of the hollowed-out vegetables stopping about 1.25 cm/1/2 inch from the top. Place the reserved top of each vegetable back where it came from (so no putting the pepper top on the aubergine – they're unsociable and don't mix well!).

Pour in 250 ml/1 cup cold water into the base of the roasting pan and then cover the vegetables with foil. Bake in the preheated oven for about 1 1/2 hours, after which time remove the foil, drizzle a little olive oil over the top, season, and pop back in the oven for about 10 minutes until they take on some colour. Let them rest while you whip up some gravy!

FRESH FIGS WITH GOAT'S CURD & ORANGE
syka tirotigma kai portocali

When I'm developing a dish, I sometimes take my inspiration from the natural habitat of the ingredients. Ingrained in my mind is a scene with fig trees heavy with the burden of ripe fruit, surrounded by goats in a subdued frenzy of gobbling up every edible ruby that has fallen from the trees. What is it about goats and figs? So this is how this delicate dish came to be... The tang of soft creamy goat's curd complements the sweetness of the velvety figs. I like to fold through some Puy lentils to add a little more substance and texture to the salad, but it also gives a wonderfully earthy note. Although this makes a great small-plate *meze* dish, I tend to increase the portion size and serve this as a big sharing salad on a large platter. I do like a large platter.

100 g/3¹/2 oz. pre-cooked Puy lentils
1 orange
120 g/4¹/4 oz. mixed green salad leaves (spinach, rocket/arugula, watercress, etc.)
a small handful of fresh flat-leaf parsley
a small handful of fresh coriander/ cilantro
a dash of freshly squeezed lemon juice
12 chicory/endive leaves, halved lengthways
12 small fresh figs or 8 large
250 g/9 oz. goat's curd or soft goat's cheese if preferred
a small handful of toasted hazelnuts, sliced
salt and freshly ground black pepper
olive oil, for drizzling
Greek honey, for drizzling

SERVES 4

I use pre-cooked Puy lentils for convenience. Break up any clumps and drizzle with a little olive oil.

Cut 12 segments from the orange (see Tip below on how best to do this) and set aside. Save the rest of the orange for the dressing.

In a bowl, mix together the lentils, salad leaves and herbs, and dress with a drizzle of olive oil, a squeeze of the reserved orange and a squeeze of lemon, and a pinch of salt and pepper. Mix with your hands.

To plate up, scatter the chicory leaves over a serving dish, shake off excess dressing from the grain salad and scatter across the top of the chicory leaves, before randomly dotting the orange segments around.

Cut the figs in half or if quite large, into quarters. Place them over the top of the salad and scatter the goat's curd or goat's cheese all over.

Finish with the hazelnuts slices over the top and a drizzle of honey.

Tip: To segment the orange, with the skin on, top and tail the orange. Cut the peel away to reveal the flesh, removing any pith. Run a knife in between the membrane to remove each segment of orange.

fire

FIRE
fotia

'Come over for an early summer barbecue' was the message from my parents. I don't know why early summer was specified (as we barbecue all year round) and come to think of it, I don't know why barbecue was mentioned either – it's always a barbecue with us – it is just the means by which we cook our food whenever we can. Today, however, it is raining. The skies are grey, the air is cold so my kids understandably exclaim 'Oh! We're not having a barbecue today then?'. I shake my head indulgently, laugh knowingly and hurry them up the path. Don't they know anything yet? As we enter the garden, the smell of cooking meat wafts through the air; that unmistakable aroma of lamb on the bone slowly rotating on skewers over charcoal (NEVER gas). You hear the occasional hiss of lemon juice used to season the meat as it sparks onto the hot coals. As we swing around the corner I glimpse the boldly striped blue and white parasol first, fat raindrops bouncing off the top of it as plumes of smoke billow out from underneath. Then through this haze I see my dad, in his

shorts, proudly presiding over his barbecue. And I'm proud of him. But maybe we'll eat inside today...

Cooking over fire is in our blood. As a method of preparing food in Greek cuisine it dates back over 3,000 years, from when the Mycenaean civilisation first used clay utensils to cook skewered meats. In Cyprus today, we still traditionally cook meat on a *foukou*, a very large industrial steel trough that houses proper charcoal and wood. Either small skewers that are threaded with cubes of meat for *souvlaki* (see page 150) are used or the much larger skewers for the Cypriot speciality of *souvla*, which take large chunks of meat, most often lamb shoulder cut into fist-sized pieces still on the bone, but also pork shoulder or sometimes chicken thighs. These *souvlas* are powered by a motor that turns the skewers slowly cooking the meat evenly. Fat renders, racing around the rotating meat like lumberjacks running on floating logs, the trickling juices self-basting the meat to keep it moist and succulent and wrapped with flavour. I sometimes

use this style of Greek barbecue at large catered events and if there is a Greek in the crowd, they'll spot a fellow countryman in seconds. Before I know it, they will be enthusiastically discussing how their parents cook *souvla*. I always find that food never fails to start a conversation and bring people together.

I'm a big fan of cooking with rotisserie skewers for many reasons but mostly because I am an epicurean at heart. I enjoy drinking, eating and socializing with friends and family, so the concept of just putting food on to cook and coming back in a couple of hours to find it done to perfection appeals to my nature. But skewering meat is just one method of cooking over fire. *Kleftiko*, the most primitive form of cooking, made use of a fire pit (see pages 82–83), and nothing beats fresh octopus cooked directly over a charcoal grill, crisped up at the edges and served with a pinch of salt, a squeeze of lemon and maybe a whisper of chilli flakes. A variety of Greek sausages are also tasty when barbecued; *sheftelia* (a cinnamon-spiced sausage wrapped in pig

caul), *pastourma* (a spicy beef sausage) and, my favourite, *loukanika* (pork meat marinated in red wine and black peppercorns). Or try a whole plump white fish, stuffed with herbs and barbecued in a salt crust (see page 143) or wrapped in vine leaves to keep the flesh moist but crisp the leaves (see page 138).

Cooking with fire is primal – there is nothing as pure. People around the globe have cooked with open flames for millennia and it seems every culture has their own version of fire cooking, from the huge *asado* grills in Argentina and the *churrasco* favoured by the Brazilian gauchos, to the *hangi* rock pit of the New Zealand Maoris and the *kadi* bowls used for mass cooking at religious celebrations in India. The principle may be the same but it's the technique and ingredients that vary. But to encapsulate the flavours of Greece and Cyprus in particular, you need nothing more than a few burnt ends and smoky air as your condiment. Oh, and maybe a little salt, and drizzle of fruity olive oil and plenty of lemons for squeezing. Always the lemons...

GRILLED AUBERGINES & FETA
melitzana kai feta

This recipe is inspired by a dish my mum cooks which we all love. Like many recipes, the essence of the dish is rooted in childhood memories. Purely for aesthetic purposes, if I spot a Japanese or Chinese aubergine, (which are longer and thinner than regular aubergines) I'll use it, but they taste the same.

2 aubergines/eggplants
a pinch of dried chilli/hot red pepper flakes
a handful of freshly chopped flat-leaf parsley
200 g/7 oz. feta cheese, crumbled
freshly squeezed lemon juice, to taste
1 garlic clove, halved
salt and freshly ground black pepper
olive oil, for brushing

SERVES 4

Without topping or tailing the aubergines, slice them lengthways about 1.25 cm/¹/₂ inch thick. Brush with olive oil, season with salt and pepper and sprinkle with the chilli flakes. Grill them on a hot barbecue/outdoor grill until they are golden and softened.

Mix together the parsley and crumbled feta and season with black pepper and a little squeeze of lemon juice (about 1 teaspoon). Do this gently, you want the feta to remain crumbled so try not to man-handle it into a paste. Set aside.

Carefully turn the aubergines over, rub with the cut garlic, then top with the parsley-feta-lemon mixture. Leave to cook for another 5 minutes or until the other side has also turned golden and softened. Carefully remove from the barbecue and serve.

CHARRED COURGETTES
kolokithakia kokinista

When I have a garlic lemon dressing, I want to know it's a lemon garlic dressing. (I am not expecting to kiss anyone that hasn't eaten this with me...) The courgettes are charred a little on the barbecue and then slathered in plenty of the dressing. This is a recipe for people who don't even like courgettes, the heathens...

3 courgettes/zucchini
2 garlic cloves, crushed
a small handful of freshly chopped flat-leaf parsley
60 ml/¹/₄ cup olive oil
freshly squeezed juice of ¹/₂ lemon
salt and freshly ground black pepper

SERVES 6

Top and tail the courgettes and then cut them lengthways into slices about 1 cm/³/₈ inch thick.

Simply mix all the rest of the ingredients together and pour over the courgettes.

Shake off any excess dressing from the courgettes, saving the dressing, and place the courgettes onto a smoking hot barbecue/outdoor grill over direct heat and cook for a few minutes on each side or until they are charred.

Once cooked, transfer to a serving dish and brush over the remaining dressing. Serve immediately.

Tip: This recipe also works fabulously with fresh asparagus spears.

BARBECUED SALMON
IN SPICED YOGURT MARINADE
kypriaka baharika solomos

Here I pay tribute to the Middle Eastern influences in Cypriot cooking by combining warm spices with fresh tangy yogurt to create a wonderfully aromatic marinade for salmon. It's best to barbecue a whole side of salmon with the skin on, it stays moist for longer and the skin protects the flesh while it's cooking over the hot coals. Once cooked, I like to place the whole side of fish onto a serving board for everyone to help themselves: the only finishing touch you need is a scattering of fresh coriander and a squeeze of lime juice. Oh, and no matter how much fish you think you are going to need, cook more!

1 side of salmon (approx. 1 kg/
  2¹/₄ lb.), skin-on, de-boned
a few sprigs of fresh coriander/
  cilantro
2 limes, quartered, for squeezing

MARINADE
200 g/scant 1 cup Greek yogurt
1 teaspoon salt
¹/₂ teaspoon ground cloves
2 garlic cloves, crushed
1 tablespoon ground cumin
1 tablespoon ground coriander
1 tablespoon paprika
1 teaspoon chilli/chili powder
1 teaspoon ground cinnamon
2 tablespoons grated fresh ginger
1 teaspoon ground turmeric
2 tablespoons olive oil

TO SERVE
a simple tomato and cucumber
  salad with flat-leaf parsley

a fish grill basket/cage for use on
  a barbecue (optional)

SERVES 6–8

Light a barbecue/outdoor grill and ensure it is hot.

Simply combine all of the marinade ingredients and paste the mixture over the flesh side of the salmon.

Enclose the salmon in a fish grill basket and place skin-side down over direct heat on the barbecue for about 12–15 minutes or until the flesh starts to turn opaque around the edges and the skin is charred. You are cooking the salmon almost two-thirds done skin-side down, using the skin to protect the flesh of the salmon whilst cooking and keep it moist.

Turn the salmon over and cook it flesh-side down for a further 5 minutes. Take it off the heat (you can check if it's cooked at this stage).

Use a fish slice to remove the salmon from the fish basket and place it on a chopping board. Scatter the fresh coriander over the top and offer lime wedges on the table for squeezing.

Tip: You can cook the salmon in your oven, if you like. You won't get the charred flavour of the barbecue, but you also won't have to stand in the rain. Pop the marinated salmon onto an oiled roasting pan and then into a preheated oven at 200°C (400°F) Gas 6 for 12–15 minutes or until cooked all the way through.

SEABASS IN VINE LEAVES WITH HERB STUFFING
labraki tiligmeno se fylla ambeliou

Wrapping seabass in vine leaves protects this delicate fish from the harsh heat of a charcoal grill; instead the flesh is gently steamed inside its wrapping, keeping it deliciously succulent. Combine that soft flesh with a light and zesty stuffing, and a crisp, almost blackened coat of arms, and you'll have a new favourite summer fish dish to enjoy.

6 large vine leaves in brine
4 tablespoons freshly chopped
    coriander/cilantro
2 tablespoons freshly chopped
    flat-leaf parsley
1 tablespoon freshly chopped basil
1/2 garlic clove, crushed
a pinch of ground cardamom
a pinch of sugar
2 tablespoons olive oil, plus extra
    for oiling
4 fresh seabass fillets, any
    pin-bones removed
salt
freshly squeezed lemon juice,
    to serve

TO SERVE (OPTIONAL)
steamed baby courgette/zucchini
    tossed in freshly chopped dill

SERVES 2

Rinse the vine leaves in clean water to wash away the brine, then leave them to soak in clean cold water until ready to use.

Mix the chopped coriander, parsley and basil with the garlic, ground cardamom, sugar and olive oil. You should have a fairly thick paste.

Lay two of the seabass fillets skin-side down on a chopping board. Paste the herb mixture over the flesh, dividing it evenly between the two. Top with the matching seabass fillets skin-side up to create two seabass 'sandwiches'.

Shake off the water from the vine leaves and cut away the thick stalk at the bottom. Lay out three of the vine leaves so they slightly overlap. Lay one fish 'sandwich' on the vine leaves and wrap the leaves around the fish. Repeat with the remaining vine leaves and the other fish 'sandwich'.

Heat a barbecue/outdoor grill until it's hot. Lightly oil the exterior of the vine leaves and place the fish parcels on the grill, seam-side down. Cook for about 5 minutes, then carefully turn over and cook for a further 5 minutes.

Once cooked, let the fish rest for a few moments and then dress with a squeeze of lemon juice and a pinch of salt (use sea salt if you have it), and serve with a glass of chilled dry white wine.

Tip: This can be cooked under a hot grill/broiler. Just place on a foil-lined grill tray and cook for 8 minutes, carefully turning halfway through the cooking time.

COD WITH KALAMATA OLIVES
WRAPPED IN DRY-CURED HAM
gados me elies kalamon tyligmenos
mes zambo stegno

Cod loin is a clean-tasting, meaty white fish and here it works beautifully complemented by the sharpness of crushed Kalamata olives and salty dry-cured ham. I enjoy cooking large cuts of fish or meat that are served whole at the table so that everyone can help themselves, and this is no exception!

750 g/1 lb. 10 oz. cod loin
a good pinch of sumac
a pinch of ground cumin
a small handful of basil leaves
**   (Greek basil if available)**
about 8 slices (or enough to wrap
**   the cod) dry-cured ham (such as**
**   Parma or Serrano)**
olive oil, for cooking and drizzling
freshly chopped flat-leaf parsley,
**   to garnish**
1 lemon, quartered, to serve

MARINADE
65 g/¹/₂ cup Kalamata olives,
**   pitted and very finely chopped**
freshly squeezed juice of ¹/₄ lemon
1 tablespoon olive oil
¹/₂ garlic clove, finely chopped
6 ripe tomatoes, deseeded and
**   diced**
salt and freshly ground black
**   pepper**

a sheet of baking parchment,
**   lightly oiled**

SERVES 4

Combine all of the prepared marinade ingredients except the tomatoes. Slowly add the tomatoes bit by bit to the olive mixture, tasting for balance of flavours; you want it salty from the olives, fresh from the lemon, with a little heat from the garlic and just balanced with sweet tomatoes. Lightly dust the cod with the sumac and cumin, then paste the marinade over the top of the fish until it is covered. Scatter over the basil leaves. (Any unused marinade that hasn't touched the fish, can be reserved for serving.)

Take the sheet of prepared baking parchment. Lay the pieces of ham side by side on it, slightly overlapping them until you have created a large 'sheet' of ham about the same length as the fish. Place the fish, marinade-side up, along the length of this 'ham sheet', and about two-thirds down it.

Lift a short side of the ham sheet up onto the fish, then roll the whole thing over away from you so that the marinade-side of the fish is now at the bottom. Fold over the remaining ham so the fish is fully enclosed, but don't worry about the ends being open.

Heat a barbecue/outdoor grill and oil the rack. When it is hot, use your hands to lightly cover the fish parcel in oil, then place the parcel seam-side down onto the rack and leave it alone! Let it cook for 5–6 minutes or until the ham is crispy, and then carefully turn it a quarter turn (going with the seam not against it, otherwise it can unfold a little). Cook the three other sides for 3–4 minutes, then remove it and let it rest.

Place on a chopping board, drizzle with olive oil and scatter with parsley. Carve at the table and serve with lemon wedges and reserved marinade.

Tip: This also works well cooked in the oven; simply place the fish parcel on an oiled sheet of baking parchment and cook in a preheated oven at 200°C (400°F) Gas 6 for 20–25 minutes.

HALLOUMI WITH HONEY & BLACK SESAME
halloumi me meli kai mauvro sesami

Halloumi is a Cypriot cheese that is delicious when simply fried or grilled. It is a medium-hard cheese and if cooked too slow or over a low heat it dries out quickly and just isn't nice. Getting the job done well relies on three basic rules: cook it from room temperature; cut it into thick slices; and cook it fast over a high heat to ensure you get that lovely charred crust but keep a soft, moist centre.

500 g/1 lb. 2 oz. good-quality halloumi cheese
4 tablespoons Greek honey
1 tablespoon black sesame seeds
olive oil, for cooking

SERVES 8

Take the halloumi out of the fridge about 30 minutes before you want to cook it to bring it to room temperature. Cut the halloumi into thick slices, at least 2.5 cm/1 inch thick, and wipe over a little olive oil, just to prevent it sticking to your grill.

Once your barbecue/outdoor grill is really hot, place the halloumi straight onto the grill – you should hear it sizzle. After about a minute, or as soon as it chars, turn the halloumi over to cook the other side. Once done, put it straight onto a serving dish, arranging the slices next to each other rather than piling them up.

Drizzle over the honey and then sprinkle over the black sesame seeds. Serve immediately and enjoy.

Tip: This works just as well cooked in a really hot cast iron frying pan/skillet.

WHIPPED GARLIC POTATOES
skordalia

A wickedly garlicky puréed mashed potato dip, rich with lashings of olive oil that is served at room temperature: be warned, this can become quite addictive! Don't mistake this for a pile of mashed potatoes, it's far richer than that. It can be enjoyed as a dip, best eaten with toasted pita, but it also works as an accompaniment with grilled fish, meat or vegetables.

400 g/14 oz. Cyprus potatoes, peeled
1/2 tablespoon crushed garlic
100 ml/1/3 cup olive oil
freshly squeezed lemon juice, to taste
a pinch of freshly chopped flat-leaf parsley
salt

SERVES 6

Cut the potatoes into large pieces and cook in salted boiling water for about 15–20 minutes or until there is no resistance when pierced with a knife.

Drain and let them steam dry for a few minutes before lightly mashing them. Add the garlic, which should be crushed down to a paste (ideally in a pestle and mortar) and mix through. Start adding the olive oil a little at a time, mashing well between each addition.

Once the potatoes are thoroughly mashed, use a hand whisk to beat them as you add the remaining olive oil and a few drops of lemon juice as you go, just to taste.

Season generously with salt and whisk through the finely chopped parsley.

SALTED SEA BREAM WITH LEMONGRASS & THYME
tsipoura alatismeni me lemonias-grasithe
kai thymari

I always feel that at the heart of Cypriot and Greek food is its respect and appreciation of incredibly fresh produce, simply cooked. This recipe is a prime example of that ethos. Buy the freshest sea bream you can source, preferably from a sun-wizened Greek fisherman standing on the edge of his boat in his ripped shorts and smoking a cigarette. Failing that, my advice is take the time to get to know your local fishmonger.

4 whole sea bream, gutted (ask your fishmonger to do this)
a handful of fresh thyme sprigs
4 lemongrass stalks
100 g/^{1}/2 cup sea salt flakes
olive oil, for oiling and drizzling

DRESSING
1 stalk lemongrass
a few drops of freshly squeezed lemon juice
1 garlic clove, crushed
a handful of freshly chopped flat-leaf parsley
a pinch of dried chilli/hot red pepper flakes (optional)
olive oil, as required (see method)

TO SERVE (see Tip, right)
charred lemon halves, for squeezing (optional)
charred Baby Gem (optional)

SERVES 4

Cut two diagonal slits in the flesh of each fish on one side. Push a couple of sprigs of thyme into each slit, then repeat on the other side. Push a lemongrass stalk through the mouth of the fish, so it goes all the way through into the cavity of the fish, then fill each fish with the remaining thyme.

Lightly oil each fish and sprinkle half the salt over one side of the fish, do the same for the other side. You're not going to be eating the salt, so add more if they are not well coated.

Place the prepared fish onto the preheated barbecue/outdoor grill over direct medium heat for about 5–6 minutes, or until the fish is charred. Use a fish knife or spatula to turn the fish over – turn them top-side down, so the stuffing doesn't fall out. Cook for another 5–6 minutes until cooked through. Remove the fish and place onto a large chopping board.

To make the dressing, peel off a few leaves from the lemongrass stick, then finely chop the centre. Add a small squeeze of lemon juice, the garlic, a little olive oil and enough finely chopped parsley to create a thick dressing (a pinch of chilli flakes wouldn't go amiss here either). Serve the fish with the dressing.

Tip: Halve some lemons, arrange them cut-side down on the rack of your hot barbecue just to char. Serve them with the fish for squeezing. You can do the same with some Baby Gem lettuce, just to serve on the side, if liked.

SKEWERED GOAT'S CHEESE, DATE & PANCETTA PARCELS
tyri ageladas, finikia kai pancenta themada

These little bundles – containing molten goat's cheese cushioning a sweet, warm date, wrapped tightly in a salty pancetta duvet – are a delight. Skewered and interwoven with charred chunks of bread, these do well to be served one skewer per person, but I like making a large pile of them for everyone to help themselves. I prefer to cook these on the barbecue, but if it's raining (and you're not Greek and not willing to stand under an umbrella next to glowing charcoals in all weathers) they do equally well under an indoor grill. I don't say that for effect, many times I've found my dad outside in the pouring rain standing next to our barbecue/outdoor grill holding a brolly – and I love you for it Paps!

450 g/1 lb. semi-soft goat's cheese log (La Bûche is very good)
12 pitted dates
12 rashers/slices of pancetta
1 small loaf bread
1 tablespoon dried oregano
a pinch of dried chilli flakes/hot red pepper flakes
salt and freshly ground black pepper
olive oil, for drizzling

12 skewers (if wooden, soak in water for 30 minutes first to avoid them catching and burning, if liked)

TO SERVE (OPTIONAL)
flat-leaf parsley
finely sliced red onion

SERVES 6

Cut the goat's cheese into 12 discs each about 5 cm/2 inches thick, and then gently push one date into the middle of each disc of cheese.

Lay a rasher of pancetta on a flat surface and then place one piece of cheese near the top. Start to wrap the pancetta around the cheese, turning the pancetta by 90 degrees halfway to create an almost-sealed parcel. Season with a little black pepper and then repeat until all the parcels are done.

Now for the croutons. Rip the bread into similar-sized pieces as the goat's cheese parcels, and drizzle some olive oil over, followed by a little seasoning, the oregano and chilli flakes.

Skewer the goat's cheese parcels and bread, alternating between the two. Try to pierce the skewer through the centre of the goat's cheese, ideally going through the date and, if possible, the end of the piece of pancetta to help hold it all together.

Place the skewers on the preheated hot barbecue/outdoor grill, turning them every few minutes until the pancetta starts to crisp.

Serve while they are warm and the cheese is molten.

BUTTERFLIED LEG OF LAMB WITH FIERY TZATZIKI
petalouda tou arniou me tsilli tallatourri

There is theatre and fun in large whole cuts of meat being cooked outdoors, but also logic. The meat stays moist and tender, it is carved on the table and brings an honesty to the food. It's just a beautiful and delicious cut of meat cooked in one of the most primal ways possible, with nothing more than plenty of seasoning. Meat always needs to rest both before and after cooking – I can't emphasize this enough – and never cook it straight out of the fridge.

2 kg/4$^{1}/_{2}$ lb. butterflied leg of lamb (boned weight, ask your butcher to butterfly the leg for you)
500 g/2$^{1}/_{4}$ cups Greek yogurt
a pinch of ground cumin
a pinch of sugar
3 lemons
1 tablespoon chilli/chili paste*
plenty of salt and freshly ground black pepper

SERVES 10

* To make a chilli/chili paste, if not using store-bought, finely chop 1 fresh red chilli/chile, dust it in salt then using the flat side of a knife, scrape it into a paste and mix it with a tablespoon of olive oil.

A leg of lamb is a hefty piece of meat and needs a good hour sitting outside the fridge to get it up to room temperature. Season it generously with salt and pepper; at least a tablespoon of both on each side.

When you are ready to cook, place the lamb skin-side down onto the hot barbecue/outdoor grill over direct heat. Quite quickly it will start to flare but that's okay, just move it away from the flames or turn it over, and then once the flames die down, turn it back over. This will happen a few times and eventually stop when most of the fat under the skin has rendered – but enjoy it! It's part of the fun of cooking outside. Cook the skin side for about 15 minutes. You want a nice dark charring to the skin side and you want to cook this fairly quickly. The whole thing should be cooked in about 30–45 minutes, depending on heat, thickness of the meat, the wind, etc.

Once the skin side has stopped flaring and has a deep crust, flip it over and let the flesh side cook for a good 10–15 minutes. I don't use a meat thermometer (although if you do, aim for about 60°C/140°F), just give it a poke with your finger and, when it feels firm with a tiny bit of give, remove it from the heat, cover loosely in foil and let it rest for 20–30 minutes. I carve this at the table.

To make the Fiery Tzatziki, mix the Greek yogurt with the cumin, sugar and a pinch of salt. Halve one of the lemons and squeeze a teaspoon or so of lemon juice into the yogurt and mix thoroughly. Swirl in the chilli paste. Serve on the side for people to help themselves to, along with the remaining lemons cut into wedges for squeezing.

SKEWERED GRILLED MEATS
souvlaki

Souvlaki are small pieces of meat cooked on skewers. They are the epitome of Greek barbecues. *Souvlaki* are commonly served in pita bread with salad and *tzatziki*. At home, however, we just pile them in a bowl and have them as part of a larger meal. Serving *souvlaki* in the Michaels' household has a very particular technique... you spoon a huge heap onto your plate and then, if you suspect you have just under-served yourself by one piece, pick another out with your fingers and stick it straight into your mouth...

Traditionally, they are made with pork, chicken or lamb, but the possibilities for combinations are endless. Try cubed fish, vegetables, cheese or even fresh fruit. The secret to cooking meat *souvlaki* is to cook them fast and cook them on a high heat; small chunks of meat can easily dry out if they are overcooked. My recipes vary by ingredients, but the cooking method remains the same for all of them. You can use metal or wooden skewers or even strong twigs of rosemary to skewer the meat – personally, I like metal, but have used all three at some time or other.

PORK SOUVLAKI
hirino souvlaki

A good cut of pork, cooked over charcoal, with the fat dripping onto the coals creating bursts of smoke, is all that's needed to create flavour here, just add a squeeze of lemon and a sprinkle of salt. Pork shoulder is a great cut for *souvlaki*, however, if you enjoy a little rendered fat, pork belly is magic.

800 g/1 lb. 12 oz. pork shoulder or pork belly, skin removed
a generous pinch of dried Greek oregano
freshly squeezed juice of 1 lemon
salt
olive oil, for drizzling

metal skewers, or wooden skewers soaked in water 30 minutes first

SERVES 4

Cut the pork into bite-sized chunks and drizzle a little olive oil over them, followed by a pinch of oregano and salt. Skewer the pork. Get a barbecue/ outdoor grill really hot.

Place the skewers of meat over direct heat and leave for a minute until the meat starts to char before turning them over. Continue turning until all sides are cooked, squeezing a little lemon juice over the pork skewers as they cook. The Greeks tend to like their meat well done, but I prefer mine a little less done. Once cooked, allow to rest, then finish with another squeeze of lemon juice and a pinch of salt.

SPICY CHICKEN SOUVLAKI
kotopoulo piperoriza kai skordo souvlaki

This isn't a traditional chicken souvlaki recipe, but the ginger and garlic paste brings a nice sharpness and depth of flavour to the chicken as it cooks over the charcoal.

2 garlic cloves, crushed
7.5-cm/3-inch piece of fresh ginger, finely grated
1 fresh red chilli/chile, very finely chopped
2 large boneless chicken breasts, meat cut into bite-sized chunks
salt and freshly ground black pepper
olive oil, for drizzling
freshly squeezed juice of 1 lemon, to serve

metal skewers, or wooden skewers soaked in water for 30 minutes first

SERVES 4

To make the marinade, pound the garlic into a smooth paste, add the ginger and chilli, and mix them all together with a small drizzle of olive oil. (Alternatively just whizz the whole lot together in a blender.) Put the chicken chunks in a large bowl and add the marinade. Use your hands to massage the marinade into the chicken. Cover and leave for 30 minutes.

To cook, skewer the chicken cubes. They should be touching each other, but not squashed; a bit of space allows the chicken to cook more quickly and keeps it moist. Get a barbecue/outdoor grill really hot. Place the skewers of chicken over direct heat and leave for a minute until the chicken starts to char before turning them over. Continue turning (rotisserie-style) until all sides are cooked, then remove the skewers from the barbecue and rest for a few minutes before serving. Finish with a squeeze of lemon juice.

YOGURT-MARINATED LAMB SOUVLAKI
arni marinarismeno me yiaourti souvlaki

Marinating the lamb in a spicy yogurt mixture not only helps tenderize the meat, but also imparts a great flavour when cooking.

4 tablespoons Greek yogurt
2 garlic cloves, crushed
a generous pinch of oregano
a generous pinch of ground cumin
800 g/1 lb. 12 oz. lamb leg, meat cut into bite-sized chunks
salt and freshly ground black pepper
olive oil, for drizzling
freshly squeezed juice of 1 lemon, to serve

metal skewers, or wooden skewers soaked in water 30 minutes first

SERVES 4

In a large bowl, mix the yogurt, crushed garlic, oregano, cumin, 1 teaspoon salt, a few grinds of pepper and a drizzle of olive oil. Add the lamb chunks to the bowl and use your hands to massage the marinade into the meat so it is fully coated. Cover and leave for at least 30 minutes or overnight if possible.

To cook, skewer the lamb cubes, shaking off the excess marinade, but leaving them lightly coated. Get a barbecue/outdoor grill really hot. Unlike the other souvlaki methods, when you place the lamb on the grill over direct heat, you can leave it for a few minutes until charred, before turning it only a couple of times. Once cooked, let the lamb rest for a few minutes, then finish with a little squeeze of lemon juice and a pinch of salt.

sundowners

SUNDOWNERS
thysi iliou

Most of my food influences stem from early memories of being surrounded by my family and wrapped in a warm security blanket of love... but not so much in this chapter, part of which stems from some hazy memories of under-age drinking painted on a canvas of neon lights, and I have a burning confession to make. Many years ago on one of our family trips to Cyprus, I was really (really) unwell one morning. Complaining of an upset stomach, the collective defence of all my older cousins (I will refrain from mentioning any names, Nikos...) and myself was; 'Oh, it must have been the fish soup!'. And we have all stuck to that story fervently for several decades now. If the recipe for fish soup consists of copious Cypriot brandy sours, B52s and *zivania* shots being imbibed into the small hours in the company of girls far too old for me, then yes, it was most definitely the fish soup! My adolescent misadventures aside, a well-made cocktail or a fiery sipper can be a wonderful thing (in moderation) so here's hoping that the cocktail recipes I've selected to share here will keep you company on many a lazy afternoon (and perhaps a few wicked nights out).

As with the food of Greece and Cyprus, the drinks and liquors are born out of the traditions of each region and the ingredients that are found there. Whether it is *ouzo*, the anise-flavoured spirit served neat on the rocks or with a splash of water to invoke the alchemy of the clear liquid turning white and cloudy, or the famed Cypriot Brandy Sour cocktail, which varies in form and sophistication. I've probably enjoyed it the most on the beach, casually made with a few glugs of brandy, a dash of bitters and topped with clear sparkling lemonade. And let's not forget a shot of *zivania*, the clear Cypriot brandy that gives any good eye-popping moonshine a run for its money!

With this brandy, often comes the coffee. In fact, a meal rarely ends without a coffee; not a skinny-chai-macchiato-with-soy-foam, but a proper coffee, a Greek coffee – coal-black and so thick that the teaspoon stands to attention. It is made in a *briki*, the traditional stove-top pot, ornate, decoratively chased and just big enough to make only a few cups. The coffee itself is a powder-fine grind and brewed very gently, so making it is a slow process. If you haven't had a Greek (or Turkish)

coffee before, be aware that you must declare your preference at the start as the sugar is added during the brewing process, not afterwards. The choice is normal, medium or sweet. I choose *medrio* (medium) which is a little bit sweet with just enough sugar to take the edge off the bitterness. Once poured into the small *demitasse* cup, a thick layer of sediment will slowly drop down to eventually sit at the bottom of the small brown sea. A glass of water on the side is mandatory and it is acceptable to pour a few drops of it into the coffee to help the sediment find its eventual resting place. The arrival of this coffee always cries out for something sweet to partner it with.

Traditional Greek desserts are small, incredibly sweet, rich and fragrant. Just one bite, or possibly two, they often arrive on spoons or sometimes a small saucer. Probably the most uniquely Greek of all these sweet treats are *glyko*, which are preserved 'spoon sweets', offered as a symbol of hospitality but usually in our house devoured on sight, with or without guests. Stewed in sugar syrup and preserved, these are most often figs, walnuts and citrus rinds, but really any fruit

or nut can be used. Every Greek island has its own speciality too – on Ikaria you will find sour cherry, Chios they use lemon blossoms, and on Naxos quince, a fruit so bitter that it can't be eaten raw. Rose petal spoon sweets are popular gifts for weddings and baptisms. Silky and seductive on the palate, once bottled these treats will keep for months. Also very popular is *baklava*. Chopped pistachios coated in a thick sugar syrup are layered between sheets of buttery filo and scored into diamonds or squares in the pan – so sticky and dense that one really is enough. Or *galombrama*, a moist semolina cake swimming in an indulgent cinnamon-infused syrup and topped with an almond. One of my favourites is *galatoboureko* (see page 166) – rich saffron custard topped and tailed with crisp filo. Some of my recipes are a gentle shift of traditional ideas and others are new creations inspired by traditional ingredients. All of them are about offering just a bite of something sweet to satisfy a craving. And I often wonder if this habit of offering just a small bite of something sweet and rich and not a piled-high plate contributes to the healthy balance in Greek cuisine.

LONG OUZO SOUR
ouzo xino makri

A take on the traditional brandy sour found in Cyprus, a refreshing long drink perfect for sipping on a lazy day basking in the sunshine.

50 ml/1³/4 fl oz. ouzo
30 ml/1 fl oz. freshly squeezed lemon juice
a dash of Angostura bitters
1 teaspoon white sugar or 15 ml/1 tablespoon
    sugar syrup (see below)
well-chilled soda water/club soda, to top up
lemon peel twists, to garnish
ice cubes, to serve

MAKES 1

Put the ouzo, lemon juice, Angostura bitters and sugar syrup or sugar into a cocktail shaker and shake to combine. Fill a highball glass with ice cubes and pour over the cocktail. Top up with soda and garnish with a couple of twists of lemon peel. Serve immediately.

Tip: To make a simple sugar syrup, add equal volumes of water and white sugar together in a small, high-sided saucepan and set over a medium heat. Gently bring to the boil until the sugar has dissolved. Reduce the heat, simmer for a few minutes to thicken and then remove from the heat and allow to cool. Once cool, pour into a screwtop jar and use as needed. The syrup will keep for up to 3 weeks in the fridge if kept airtight.

SHORT OUZO SOUR
ouzo xino mikro

If you're looking for a reviving smack around the chops, this is the one for you. A Greek take on a classic short and sour cocktail.

60 ml/2 fl oz. ouzo
30 ml/1 fl oz. freshly squeezed lemon juice
1 teaspoon white sugar or 15 ml/1 tablespoon
    sugar syrup (see below left)
1 egg white (from a very fresh egg)
green olive, to serve
ice cubes, to shake and serve

MAKES 1

Put the ouzo, lemon juice, sugar or sugar syrup and egg white into a cocktail shaker half-filled with ice cubes and shake vigorously for 15–20 seconds until the shaker frosts.

Strain into an ice cube-filled old-fashioned/rocks glass and garnish with a green olive skewered on a cocktail stick/toothpick. Serve immediately.

WATERMELON MARTINI WITH MASTIHA
karpouzi martini me masticha

Watermelon juice mixed with the unique flavour of Chios Mastiha makes for an aromatic and somewhat historical summer cocktail. Chios Mastiha gets its unique flavour from the resin of the mastic tree, known as 'tears'. Mysteriously, mastic trees grow worldwide, but only the mastic trees in Chios will weep and produce this resin.

1 teaspoon freshly squeezed lemon juice
1 teaspoon white sugar
60 ml/2 fl oz. watermelon juice (see tip)
60 ml/2 fl oz. Chios Mastiha
slice of watermelon, to garnish
ice cubes, to shake

MAKES 1

Put the lemon juice and sugar into a cocktail shaker and stir with a bar spoon until the sugar has dissolved.

Add a few ice cubes and pour in the watermelon juice and Mastiha. Shake until the shaker frosts. Pour into a Martini glass and garnish the rim with a small wedge of watermelon. Serve immediately.

Tip: 180 g/6^1/$_2$ oz. cubes of watermelon flesh should yield about 100 ml/^{1}/$_3$ cup juice. Place the flesh of the watermelon (no need to deseed it) into the cup of a blender and blitz it. Pass it through a fine sieve/strainer into a jug/pitcher to remove the seeds and any lumps and leave you with smooth juice. Keep it covered and refrigerated and use it on the same day it is made.

BRANDY SUNBURN
koniak iliako-enkavma

Quite possibly my new favourite cocktail. A little sharp, a little sweet, a little bitter. I call this the Brandy Sunburn because you won't feel any pain until it's too late...

30 ml/1 fl oz. Greek brandy
10 ml/2 teaspoons pomegranate molasses, plus extra to serve
1 teaspoon sugar syrup (see below left)
a dash of Angostura bitters
well-chilled soda water/club soda, to top up
pomegranate seeds, to garnish
ice cubes, to shake and serve

MAKES 1

Put the brandy, pomegranate molasses and sugar syrup in a cocktail shaker and add a dash of bitters.

Add a few ice cubes and shake until the shaker frosts. Pour into an ice-filled tumbler and top up with soda water.

Garnish with a few pomegranate seeds and add a small drizzle of pomegranate molasses over the top. Serve immediately.

OUZO & MINT GRANITA
ouzo kai granite mentas

I created this recipe years ago for the opening night of my first ever pop-up restaurant. It was such a hit, it's been on the menu ever since. The combination of mint, sugar and lime with a hint of ouzo, all wrapped up in shaved ice, is just divine. Best served in a small tumbler whilst watching the sunset...

125 g/scant ^{2}/3 cup caster/
   granulated sugar
25 g/1^1/4 cups fresh mint leaves,
   stalks removed, plus extra
   to decorate
freshly squeezed juice of 4 limes
   (about 120 ml/^{1}/2 cup)
freshly squeezed juice of ^{1}/2 lemon
   (about 30 ml/2 tablespoons)
75 ml/5 tablespoons ouzo
a pinch of salt

2-litre/quart lidded, freezerproof
   container
20 small glasses or tumblers
   (see Tip, right)

MAKES 20 SERVINGS

Place all the ingredients into a blender with 850 ml/3^1/2 cups of water and a pinch of salt. Pulse until the mint leaves are pulverized and the sugar has dissolved. (Do not blend the mint stalks or seeds from the lemon and limes, as it can make the finished granita bitter.) Also be aware that if you add too much ouzo, the alcohol will stop the granita from freezing. Taste for balance of flavours, remembering that they will dull slightly once frozen.

Pass the mixture through a sieve/strainer and into the freezerproof container. Place the container in the freezer for 6 hours, then remove it from the freezer and break up the semi-frozen mixture with a fork. Place back in the freezer, this time for at least 24 hours.

To serve, scrape the length of the frozen mixture with a fork to create a 'snow' and quickly spoon it into the glasses. Decorate with a few small fresh mint leaves. Serve immediately with teaspoons.

Tip: Pop your serving glasses into the freezer and use them frosted to help keep the granita frozen for as long as possible once it is served.

ROSE PETAL RIZOGALO WITH PISTACHIOS
tetalo triantafyllou rizogalo me fystikia

Rizogalo translates as rice (*rizi*) and milk (*galo*) and is alive in the childhood memories of every Greek I've ever met. An amalgamation of a few simple ingredients creates a sweet indulgence that has been enjoyed by generations. I've kept the ingredients list minimal, letting the starch from the rice create the creamy texture, and given it a fresh summery note with rose water and a sprinkle of crushed pistachios. The nature of this dish means it can take a little more or less liquid when cooking, just depending on the rice, the heat, etc. so keep extra milk on standby just in case you need it to loosen the texture.

190 g/1 cup Arborio rice
**50 g/¹/₄ cup caster/granulated
    sugar**
**5-cm/2-inch piece of lemon peel
    (no pith)**
**1.25 litres/5 cups full-fat/
    whole milk**
¹/₂ tablespoon rose water
**rose syrup (such as Monin),
    for drizzling**
**fresh or dried rose petals, to
    decorate (see tip)**
**2 tablespoons pistachio nuts,
    roughly chopped, to decorate**

SERVES 4

Add the rice, sugar, lemon peel and 1 litre/4 cups of the milk to a pan over a low heat. Bring to a gentle simmer and cook for 30 minutes, stirring occasionally. You need to keep an eye on this, if you don't stir it enough or have the heat too high, it will stick to the bottom of the pan.

The beautiful soft white mixture won't thicken until the last few minutes of cooking, so stay with it.

Once the rice is just about cooked (you want a little chewiness but no crunch), fold through the remaining 250 ml/1 cup of milk and remove from the heat. Give it a few minutes to cool slightly, then stir in the rose water.

You can serve this warm, or alternatively (and more traditionally), pour into heatproof, sturdy glasses and then leave to chill in the fridge. It does thicken as it sets, so if you prefer a runnier version, add a little extra milk once it's chilled to loosen.

Just before serving, drizzle over some rose syrup and scatter with rose petals and a few broken pistachio nuts to decorate.

Tip: Flowers have been used in cooking for centuries, but sadly some are poisonous so never use a floral decoration unless you are certain it is safe to. And never use petals from a flower that may have been sprayed with chemicals or pesticides. Ideally, buy culinary quality petals (these are becoming more widely available now in supermarkets) or if you use petals from the garden, wash them thoroughly before use and gently pat dry.

SAFFRON & ALMOND CUSTARD PIE
galatoboureko me safra kai amygdala

This creamy sugar syrup-soaked dessert is so indulgent and I LOVE it. I have
no willpower whatsoever where it is concerned... If I'm offered a 'doggy bag'
filled with this, I have to decline. I just know I'll eat it in one sitting as soon as
I get home. Like many Greek sweets, this goes best with strong black coffee
and passionate debate. The saffron gives the custard a lovely flavour, but go
easy with it – a little goes a long way and you don't want it to overwhelm.

CUSTARD
2 eggs plus 1 egg yolk
3 tablespoons cornflour/cornstarch
80 g/scant $^1/_2$ cup caster/
   granulated sugar
1 litre/4 cups full-fat/whole milk
a small pinch of saffron strands
   (about 6, see recipe intro)
80 g/$^1/_2$ cup semolina
30 g/2 tablespoons butter
a few drops of pure vanilla extract

PASTRY
200 g/1$^3/_4$ sticks butter, melted
225 g/8 oz. filo/phyllo pastry
   (see Tip on Filo on page 34)
salt

CINNAMON SYRUP
200 g/1 cup caster/granulated
   sugar
250 ml/1 cup cold water
1 cinnamon stick
a few drops of freshly squeezed
   lemon juice

TO DECORATE
a handful of flaked/sliced almonds,
   toasted

*a 33 x 23-cm/13 x 9-inch baking
   pan, greased*

SERVES 12

Preheat the oven to 160°C (325°F) Gas 3.

Start by making the custard. Whisk together the eggs, egg yolk,
cornflour and sugar with a little of the cold milk until you have a creamy
paste. Set aside.

Put the saffron and the remaining milk, the semolina, butter and vanilla
extract in a pan and bring to the boil, then turn off the heat and let it cool
a little. Add a little of the hot milk mixture to the egg paste, whisking as
you do. Keep doing this until you have added about 250 ml/1 cup of hot
milk mixture to the eggs, then tip the egg mixture into the rest of the hot
milk mixture, whisking as you do. Heat this gently, stirring all the time,
until it starts to thicken, then remove from the heat and let it cool.

Now for the pastry. Have your prepared baking pan, melted butter,
pastry brush and a palette knife in front of you. Roll out a sheet of filo just
big enough to fit snugly inside the pan. Brush the pastry with melted
butter. Continue layering pastry and brushing with butter until you have
about five layers. Now gently pour in the cooled custard, smoothing it out
if needed. To top the pie, do as you did for the base until you have five
layers of buttered filo. For the final layer, brush it with butter and sprinkle
with a little salt.

Bake in the preheated oven for 1 hour and then remove. Make a few
incisions in the pastry with a knife (this will help the syrup weave its way
in when you add it) and let it cool.

To make the cinnamon syrup, put the sugar, water and cinnamon stick
in a pan and bring to a simmer. Let it bubble for a minute, then turn off the
heat. Add a little lemon juice and, once it's stopped bubbling, pour it over
the pie. Sprinkle with the flaked almonds and leave to cool for at least an
hour before cutting into squares to serve.

GREEK MESS WITH ORANGE BLOSSOM MERINGUE
elliniko chaos me triantafylla portocalias marenkes

My Greek-inspired take on the British classic Eton Mess, and one that I personally love. Lots of sharp, tangy berry flavour, smothered in a cloud of creamy Greek yogurt. I've added a little orange blossom water to the meringue mixture to give it a floral note in keeping with the summer vibe of this recipe. If you can't be bothered to make your own meringues, buy good-quality ready-made mini ones and I promise no one will know your dirty secret. Except me... But I'll forgive you if you let me have two.

MERINGUE
3 egg whites
**120 g/generous ¹/₂ cup caster/
    superfine sugar**
1 teaspoon orange blossom water

RASPBERRY COULIS
250 g/2 cups fresh raspberries
**1 tablespoon caster/granulated
    sugar**
**a few drops of freshly squeezed
    lemon juice**

TO FINISH
**150 g/scant 1¹/₄ cups fresh
    blackberries**
500 g/2¹/₄ cups Greek yogurt

*1–2 baking sheets, lined with
    baking parchment*
4 glass tumblers

SERVES 4

Preheat the oven to 120°C (250°F) Gas ¹/₂.

The meringue recipe will make over double what you need, but they store well and last for ages. I say if you're going to the trouble of making meringues, you might as well make a few extra!

Start by whisking the egg whites until you have soft, white peaks. A little at a time, add the sugar into the egg whites, beating continuously. I highly recommend an electric hand whisk for this, and that is based on personal experience. Continue whisking until all the sugar is fully incorporated, then whisk in the orange blossom water.

Dollop about 24 heaped dessertspoons of meringue onto the lined baking sheet(s) leaving plenty of space between them. Bake in the preheated oven for 1 hour, then turn off the heat and leave them to cool inside the oven. (Or take them out and let them cool on a wire rack if you want them a little chewy, but they work best crisp for this recipe.)

For the coulis, blend the raspberries with the sugar and lemon juice, then pass through a sieve/strainer to remove the seeds. Set aside.

To finish, cut all the blackberries in half, saving four whole ones to decorate. Fold the halved blackberries into the yogurt. Break up some meringues and layer each tumbler with their share of the pieces, followed by the coulis and yogurt. Keep layering, in no particular order, before reaching the top of the tumbler. Finish with one whole blackberry, a final drizzle of the raspberry coulis and a sprinkle of finely crushed meringue.

Serve quite quickly otherwise the meringue will start to dissolve.

FILO 'SHARER' WITH WHIPPED CITRUS YOGURT & METAXA CHERRIES
filo kai yiaourti esperidoyides kai kerasia

I am hoping that this is a recipe that will change the way you like to eat dessert. Just bring it to the table offering spoons and no plates – this isn't designed to be cut and served, it's to be eaten all together with the filo acting as a stage on which all the other ingredients perform their flavour dance.

8 sheets filo/phyllo pastry
   (see Tip on Filo on page 34)
100 g/7 tablespoons butter, melted

METAXA CHERRIES
500 g/1 lb. 2 oz. frozen cherries,
   thawed, with their juice
a few glugs of Metaxa brandy
1 tablespoon caster/superfine
   sugar

WHIPPED CITRUS YOGURT
300 g/1¹/² cups Greek yogurt
150 g/²/³ cup mascarpone cheese
2 tablespoons icing/confectioners'
   sugar, plus extra for dusting
about 80 ml/scant ¹/³ cup freshly
   squeezed lemon juice

SWEET DUKKAH
5 ginger cookies
2 tablespoons toasted pistachios
a pinch of sugar
a pinch of ground coriander
salt and ground black pepper

TO FINISH
100 ml/¹/³ cup carob syrup
20 small fresh basil leaves

a piping/pastry bag (optional)

SERVES 8

Preheat the oven to 180°C (360°F) Gas 4.

Start by laying out a sheet of filo on a baking sheet, ensuring it sits flat. Using a pastry brush, brush the sheet with melted butter. Add another sheet of pastry on top and brush again with butter. Repeat until you've got four layers of pastry; there's no need to butter the top sheet, instead, rinse your fingers under water and lightly splash the top sheet – this keeps the pastry from burning. Bake in the preheated oven for about 15–20 minutes or until golden and crisp. Do not let it burn. Repeat with the remaining four sheets of pastry. You'll now have two sets of crisply baked pastry.

Drain the cherries and douse in a few good splashes of Metaxa and add the sugar. Leave them to steep for 30 minutes.

Meanwhile, make the whipped citrus yogurt by whisking the yogurt, mascarpone and icing sugar with a generous amount of lemon juice. Spoon into a piping/pastry bag (if using) and chill until needed.

Dukkah is a Middle Eastern spice mix but here, we're creating a sweet version. Chop or very coarsely blend the cookies, pistachios, sugar and ground coriander with a pinch of salt and a few grinds of black pepper.

Once all the components are made, you're ready to assemble the sharer. Lay the first batch of baked pastry onto a large serving board or tray and pipe (or spoon) six small dots of the yogurt on top. Drizzle over a couple of tablespoons of the cherry steeping juice – not too much, you don't want it soggy. Place the second batch of pastry on top. This time, gently make a few large cracks in it by pressing lightly with your fingers. Pipe (or spoon) 16 piles of yogurt randomly over the whole sheet. Sprinkle piles of the dukkah in-between the yogurt. Drain the cherries and dot spoonfuls in a few places. Drizzle the carob syrup across the top, scatter with basil leaves and dust lightly with icing sugar. Serve with eight spoons and a big smile.

SMOKED CHOCOLATE BAKLAVA
kapnisti chokolata baklava

Whenever I think of times I've spent in Cyprus, there are certain images that always come to mind. One of them is leathery-skinned old men playing backgammon in the street outside a café, dark bitter coffee perfuming the air and camouflaging the smoke from their cigarettes, and something sweet served on a tea saucer. This is my tribute to the memory of that scene.

100 g/^{3}/$_4$ cup walnut halves
100 g/^{3}/$_4$ cup pistachios
100 g/^{3}/$_4$ cup hazelnuts
1 teaspoon ground cinnamon
30 sheets filo/phyllo pastry (see
   Tip on Filo on page 34)
200 g/1^3/$_4$ sticks butter, melted

SMOKED CHOCOLATE SAUCE
150 g/5^1/$_2$ oz. 70% cocoa solids
   dark/bittersweet chocolate,
   broken into pieces
250 ml/1 cup double/heavy cream
1 tablespoon sugar
a pinch of salt

COFFEE SYRUP
400 g/2 cups caster/granulated
   sugar
250 ml/1 cup cold water
3 tablespoons strong freshly
   brewed espresso coffee
1 teaspoon freshly squeezed lemon
   juice

60 g/1 cup wood chips, ideally
   fruit wood, such as apple, cherry
   or maple
a 33 x 23-cm/13 x 9-inch baking
   pan, greased
4 wooden skewers

**MAKES AT LEAST 12 BUT MORE
DEPENDING ON SIZE CUT**

Prepare all your ingredients in advance before assembling. Start by coarsely grinding all the nuts with the cinnamon and set aside.

To make the smoked chocolate sauce, combine the chocolate, cream, sugar and salt and put inside a small heatproof dish. Line a frying pan/skillet with foil, put the wood chips on top and set over a high heat until the woodchips start to smoke, about 5–10 minutes. As soon as they do, lay the skewers on top to act as a mini grate. Place the chocolate dish on top and cover the whole thing in foil. Leave to smoke on a low heat for 10 minutes, then remove from the heat, cover and leave for 10 minutes.

After this time, uncover the chocolate dish and mix thoroughly with a metal spoon to create a smooth chocolate sauce. Set aside.

Cut the filo pastry to the same size as your baking pan. Place a sheet of filo inside the prepared baking pan and brush the filo with melted butter. Repeat until you have layered 10 sheets of filo. Add a layer of ground nuts. Add another five sheets of filo, brushing each layer with more butter. Pour in enough chocolate sauce to create a thin even layer over the filo, then lay another sheet on top and smooth out with your hand before buttering. Continue layering with five sheets of filo, a layer of ground nuts, five sheets of filo, a layer of chocolate sauce and finish with five sheets of filo.

To make the syrup, put the sugar, water and espresso in a high-sided saucepan over a medium heat and bring to the boil, stirring occasionally. Once it starts to boil, turn the heat to low and let it simmer gently for 5–10 minutes, until the syrup starts to thicken then set aside to cool (but not in the fridge). Cut the baklava into squares or diamonds. Flick some water over the top to stop it burning. Bake in the preheated oven for 40 minutes. Remove from the oven and immediately pour over the cooled syrup. Leave to soak at room temperature, ideally overnight but for a few hours at least.

INDEX

afelia 86
aioli, saffron 67
almonds: saffron & almond custard pie 166
apricots: pickled apricot salsa 90
arni fileto me kimino 74
arni kleftiko 82
arni kormou tis kyprou 77
arni marinarismeno me yiaourti souvlaki 151
arni tava 78
asparagus: ribbon salad 114
aubergines/eggplants: grilled aubergine & feta 132
oven-baked vegetables with harissa 118
roasted aubergine dip 24
sultry aubergines 37
avgolemoni rizoto me krotides kotopolou 89

baklava, smoked chocolate 173
beans: Cypriot slow-cooked white beans 122
giant baked beans 33
pork fillet with smoky white beans 90
smoky red mullet & white bean stew 60
beef: braised beef short ribs 81
beetroot: salt-baked beetroot 17
seared goat's cheese 22
'birds' nest' poussin 94
brandy sunburn 159
bread: flatbread 9
briam me harissa 118
broad/fava beans: stewed fine beans 121
bulgar wheat & vermicelli noodles 113

calamari *see* squid
cannellini beans: Cypriot slow-cooked white beans 122
pork fillet with smoky white beans 90
smoky red mullet & white bean stew 60

carrots: ribbon salad 114
cauliflower with tahini 37
ceviche, sea bream & watermelon 14
cheese: charred chilli & feta dip 24
courgette & feta fritters 29
creamy chicken risotto 89
feta & mint greens 102
Greek salad 109
Greek vegetable tart 110
grilled aubergine & feta 132
halloumi with honey & black sesame 142
orzo, roasted tomato & feta salad 117
prawns baked in feta & tomato sauce 63
red pepper & feta salsa 30
skewered goat's cheese, date & pancetta parcels 146
spinach & feta balls with watermelon 29
watermelon & halloumi bowls 105
see also goat's cheese
cherries: filo 'sharer' Metaxa cherries 170
chicken: creamy chicken risotto 89
spicy chicken *souvlaki* 151
ten cloves garlic lemon chicken 97
chicken livers with sherry 42
chillies/chiles: charred chilli & feta dip 24
fiery tzatziki 149
chocolate: smoked chocolate baklava 173
clams: fisherman's soup 51
seafood pasta with ouzo 48
cod: cod with kalamata olives wrapped in dry-cured ham 141
cod wrapped in *kadayif* pastry 64
coffee: smoked chocolate baklava 173
courgettes/zucchini: charred courgettes 132

courgette & feta fritters 29
Greek vegetable tart 110
oven-baked vegetables with harissa 118
ribbon salad 114
ten cloves garlic lemon chicken 97
cucumber: Greek salad 109
custard pie, saffron & almond 166
Cypriot lamb shanks 77
Cypriot roasted lamb chunks & potatoes 78
Cypriot slow-cooked white beans 122
Cyprus lemon potatoes 106

dates: skewered goat's cheese, date & pancetta parcels 146
dips 24–5
drinks 158–9

eggplants *see* aubergines
ellenike salada 109
ellenikes patates neos 106
elliniko chaos me triantafylla portocalias marenkes 169
ellinko yiaourti 8

fasolaki me nigella sporous 121
fasolia 122
fava beans *see* broad beans
fava me frigavismena baharika 25
fennel: hake 'en papillote' 64
feta cheese *see* cheese
figs with goat's curd & orange 126
filo dolmades 34
filo kai yiaourti esperidoyides kai kerasia 170
filo pastry/Phyllo pastry: filled crispy filo rolls 34
filo 'sharer' with Metaxa cherries 170
fine beans with nigella seeds 121
fish: fisherman's soup 51
seafood orzo risotto 68

flatbread 9
flower & herb salad 102
frigmeno kounoupithy kai tahini 37
fritters: courgette & feta fritters 29
crispy calamari 56
vegetable tempura 30

gados me elies kalamon tyligmenos mes zambo stegno 141
gados tiligmeno me kadeifi kai safra aioli 67
galatoboureko me safra kai amygdala 166
garitha saganaki 63
garlic: saffron aioli 67
ten cloves garlic lemon chicken 97
whipped garlic potatoes 142
see also wild garlic/ramps
gemista 125
gigante beans: giant baked beans 33
gigantes plaki 33
goat: kid goat *kleftiko* 83
goat's cheese: fresh figs with goat's curd & orange 126
seared goat's cheese with hazelnuts & honey 22
grandmother's meatballs 41
granita, ouzo & mint 162
Greek mess 169
Greek new potato salad 106
Greek salad 109
Greek vegetable tart 110

hake: fisherman's soup 51
hake 'en papillote' 64
halfway *'pastitsio'* 93
halloumi me meli kai mauvro sesami 142
ham: cod wrapped in dry-cured ham 141
harissa, oven-baked vegetables with 118
hirino fileto me verikoko salsa kai fasolia 90
hirino souvlaki 150
horta me feta kai thiosmi 102

kadayif pastry: 'bird's nest' poussin 94

cod wrapped in kadayif pastry 64
kakavia 51
kalamari stifado 52
kalamari tragano me tsilli 56
kapnisti chokolata baklava 173
karpouzi kai halloumi kypella 105
karpouzi martini me masticha 159
katsiki kleftiko 83
kid goat *kleftiko* 83
kleftiko 82–3
kolifa 21
kolokithakia kokinista 132
kolokitho-keftedes 29
koniak iliako-enkavma 159
kotopoulo folias 94
kotopoulo lemonato me skordo 97
kotopoulo piperoriza kai skordo souvlaki 151
kourkoumi mydia 57
kypriaka baharika solomos 137
kypriakes patates me lemoni 106

labraki tiligmeno se fylla ambeliou 138
lahanika tempura 30
lamb: butterflied leg of lamb with fiery tzatziki 149
Cypriot lamb shanks 77
Cypriot roasted lamb chunks & potatoes 78
filled crispy filo rolls 34
lamb shoulder *kleftiko* 82
lamb sirloin with cumin crust 74
yogurt-marinated lamb souvlaki 151
lemon: Cyprus lemon potatoes 106
hake 'en papillote' 64
lemon & thyme whitebait 57
sea bream & watermelon ceviche 14
ten cloves garlic lemon chicken 97
lemoni kai thymari maritha 57
lentils: fresh figs with goat's curd & orange 126

grilled octopus with squid ink lentils 55
limes: ouzo & mint granita 162
liver: sautéed chicken livers with sherry 42

marpouni kapnistiko me thalassika fasolia 60
martini: watermelon with Mastiha 159
mavrismene tsilli kai feta voutia 24
meatballs, grandmother's 41
melitzana kai feta 132
melitzanosalada 24
melizana me melases stafiliou 37
meringue, orange blossom 169
milk: homemade yogurt 8
rose petal rizogalo 165
miso-pastitsio 93
mussels, turmeric 57

noodles: bulgar wheat & vermicelli noodles 113
nuts: smoked chocolate baklava 173

octapothe kai kalamari mes pye fakes 55
octopus with squid ink lentils 55
olives: cod with kalamata olives 141
onions, braised beef short ribs with 81
orzo pasta: orzo, roasted tomato & feta salad 117
seafood orzo risotto 68
ouranio toxo salada me tomades 18
ouzo: long ouzo sour 158
ouzo & mint granita 162
short ouzo sour 158
ouzo kai granite mentas 162
ouzo xino makri 158
ouzo xino mikro 158

pakaliaros tiligmenos me maratho kai diatirimena lemonia 64
pancetta: skewered goat's cheese, date & pancetta parcels 146
panzariasalata 17

pasta: halfway 'pastitsio' 93
orzo, roasted tomato & feta salad 117
seafood orzo risotto 68
seafood pasta with ouzo 48
'pastitsio', halfway 93
pastries: filled crispy filo rolls 34
filo 'sharer' with Metaxa cherries 170
saffron & almond custard pie 166
smoked chocolate baklava 173
peperia kai feta salsa 30
peppers: Greek vegetable tart 110
red pepper & feta salsa 30
petalouda tou arniou me tsilli tallatourri 149
petits pois: feta & mint greens 102
Phyllo pastry see filo pastry
pickled apricot salsa 90
pita 9
pita horis zymi 9
pork: grandmother's meatballs 41
halfway 'pastitsio' 93
pork & rice-stuffed vegetables 125
pork fillet with smoky white beans 90
pork souvlaki 150
red-wine marinated pork 86
potatoes: Cypriot roasted lamb chunks & potatoes 78
Cyprus lemon potatoes 106
Greek new potato salad 106
kid goat kleftiko 83
lamb shoulder kleftiko 82
oven-baked vegetables with harissa 118
whipped garlic potatoes 142
pourgouri 113
poussin, 'bird's nest' 94
prawns/shrimp: prawns baked in feta & tomato sauce 63
seafood pasta with ouzo 48

prunes: Cypriot lamb shanks 77

quinoa: salad for the soul 21

rainbow tomato salad 18
ramps see wild garlic
raspberries: Greek mess 169
red mullet & white bean stew 60
ribbon salad 114
rice: creamy chicken risotto 89
pork & rice-stuffed vegetables 125
rose petal rizogalo 165
risotto: creamy chicken risotto 89
seafood orzo 68
rose petal rizogalo 165

saffron & almond custard pie 166
saffron aioli 67
salada agrion botanigon kai loulouthia 102
salada kritharaki me frigmenes tomades kai feta 117
salada lahaniki tarta 110
salada tis kordellas 114
salads: flower & herb salad 102
fresh figs with goat's curd & orange 126
Greek new potato salad 106
Greek salad 109
orzo, roasted tomato & feta salad 117
rainbow tomato salad 18
ribbon salad 114
salad for the soul 21
seared goat's cheese with hazelnuts & honey 22
watermelon & halloumi bowls 105
salmon, barbecued 137
salsa: pickled apricot salsa 90
red pepper & feta salsa 30
salt-baked beetroot 17
salted sea bream 143
sea bream: salted sea bream 143
sea bream &

watermelon ceviche 14
seabass: fisherman's soup 51
seabass in vine leaves 138
seafood orzo risotto 68
seafood pasta with ouzo 48
shrimp see prawns
sikodakia kotopoulou me krasi 42
skordalia 142
soup, fisherman's 51
souvlaki 150–1
spaghetti: halfway 'pastitsio' 93
spanakopita me karpouzi 29
spinach: feta & mint greens 102
hake 'en papillote' 64
spinach & feta balls with watermelon 29
split pea dip 25
squid: crispy calamari 56
fisherman's soup 51
seafood orzo risotto 68
seafood pasta with ouzo 48
slow-cooked squid 52
squid ink lentils, grilled octopus with 55
stew, smoky red mullet & white bean 60
syka tirotigma kai portocali 126

tahini, cauliflower with 37
tart, Greek vegetable 110
tempura, vegetable 30
tetalo triantafyllou rizogalo me fystikia 165
thalassika me kritharaki 68
thalassika zimarika me ouzo 48
tomatoes: Cypriot lamb shanks 77
Cypriot slow-cooked white beans 122
fisherman's soup 51
giant baked beans 33
Greek salad 109
Greek vegetable tart 110
orzo, roasted tomato & feta salad 117
prawns baked in feta & tomato sauce 63

rainbow tomato salad 18
seafood pasta with ouzo 48
slow-cooked squid 52
stewed fine beans with nigella seeds 121
tsipoura alatismeni me lemonias-grasithe kai thymari 143
tsipoura me karpouzi ceviche 14
turmeric mussels 57
tyri ageladas, finikia kai pancenta themada 146
tyri gidas me fintoukia kai meli 22
tzatziki, fiery 149

vegetables: oven-baked vegetables with harissa 118
pork & rice-stuffed vegetables 125
vegetable tempura 30
vine leaves, seabass in 138
vothino stifado me mikro-paithaki 81

watermelon: sea bream & watermelon ceviche 14
spinach & feta balls with watermelon 29
watermelon & halloumi bowls 105
watermelon martini with Mastiha 159
wheat berries: salad for the soul 21
whitebait, lemon & thyme 57
wild garlic/ramps, salt-baked beetroot with 17

yiayia's keftedes 41
yogurt: fiery tzatziki 149
homemade yogurt 8
spiced yogurt marinade 137
whipped citrus yogurt 170
yogurt-marinated lamb souvlaki 151

zucchini see courgettes

THANK YOU...

To my darling wife Anna, I never say it enough – but thank you. Thank you for always being there and putting up with me and holding our entire family together whilst I disappear to a darkened room to write my books and sometimes take a nap without telling you. Thank you for putting up with constantly being barraged with the phrase 'does this taste good' and not hitting me repeatedly, I love you, I don't know how you do it.

To my gorgeous children, Eva, Alexi and Luca, without you in the house it would be way too quiet to do any work. I love you, you bunch of cheeky monkeys.

My mum and dad, where do I begin? Without that moment in Cyprus some 40 plus years ago I wouldn't be here now, literally. So thank you for making me and making me me. Thank you for your unconditional love and time and all those home-cooked meals that my brothers Stephan, Marcus and I devoured and that have inspired my recipes. Similarly my gratitude goes to the rest of my family who have given me their time and anecdotes and memories of food...

I want to thank Julia Charles, Editorial Director, for fabulous lunches, your patience and making this gravelly toned geezer actually sound eloquent – I'm sure you have mastered the art of black magic. I also want to thank Cindy Richards Publisher who, along with Julia, immediately shared my vision of this book and believed in me. I hope to do you both proud. Or at least I think that's what's written in our contract for me to say, right?

I also owe a host of other creative people my gratitude for their unwavering help and putting up with my interference in their areas of specialism, that I know nothing of. That's you Sonya Nathoo, Leslie Harrington, Kathy Kordalis, Mowie Kay, Tony Hutchinson, David Hearn, Helen Lewis of Literally PR and my agent Susan Mears.

Finally, if you are reading this, I presume you bought a copy, thank you. If you're just flicking through whilst standing in a bookshop, honestly, this is the best cookbook ever written so I suggest you go to the till right now to buy it.

PICTURE CREDITS

All photography by Mowie Kay apart from:
pages 10–11 George Pachantouris/Getty Images
page 12l Stefan Auth/Getty Images
page 12r Michael Runkel/robertharding/Getty Images
page 13r Peter Eastland/Alamy Stock Photo
pages 44–45 efilippou/Getty Images
page 46l A. Panagiotopoulou/Getty Images
page 46r Westend61/Getty Images
page 47l Andrei Troitskiy/Getty Images
page 47r Kyle Igarashi/Getty Images
pages 70–71 Alexge Photography/EyeEm/Getty Images
page 72 Juliette Dierickx/EyeEm/Getty images
page 73l Michael Robbins/Getty Images
page 73c Carine Vaissiere/Alamy Stock Photo
pages 98–99 Brand X Pictures/Getty Images
page 100l PeopleImages/Getty Images
page 100r Westend61/Getty Images
page 101l Chris Mellor/Getty Images
page 101c Jurjen Huisman/EyeEm/Getty Images
page 101r Patricia Fenn Gallery/Getty Images
pages 128–129 Doug Pearson/Getty Images
page 130l EyesWideOpen/Getty Images
page 130r Erin Kunkel/© Ryland, Peters & Small
page 131l Marianna Massey/Getty Images
page 131c Thanasis Zovoilis/Getty Images
pages 154–155 Bruno Guerreiro/Getty Images
page 156l Emma Wood/Alamy Stock Photo
page 156r dinosmichail/Alamy Stock Photo
page 157c Melanie Acevedo/Getty Images
page 157r Ioannis Stergiopoulos/Alamy Stock Photo